Come All You Brave Soldiers

Blacks in the Revolutionary War

CLINTON COX

SCHOLASTIC INC.

New York Toronto London Auckland Sydney
Mexico City New Delhi Hong Kong Buenos Aires

ISBN 0-590-47577-0

12 11 10 9 8 7 6 5 4 3 2   3 4 5 6 7 8/0

Printed in the U.S.A.   40

First paperback printing, January 2003

For my father, Major Lafayette C. Cox, Sr. (Chaplain) and my uncle, 1st Sergeant J. D. Cox: two of the almost two million brave black soldiers who have risked their lives for this country's freedom.

PROLOGUE

"*Of the services and sufferings of the colored soldiers of the Revolution, no attempt has, to our knowledge, been made to preserve a record. Their history is not written; it lies upon the soil watered with their blood; who shall gather it? It rests with their bones in the charnel house; who shall exhume it?*"

(Abolitionist and educator Rev. William Howard Day, addressing a convention of black veterans of the War of 1812 in Cleveland, Ohio, 1852).

The birth of the United States as a result of the long and bloody Revolutionary War with Great Britain, is one of the most important events in world history. Hundreds of books have been written about it from almost every point of view; dozens of movies have shown us brave American soldiers suffering and dying in the cause of freedom; and thousands of articles have been printed in mass market magazines and academic journals.

Yet today, almost 150 years after Reverend Day spoke to the veterans in Cleveland, the role of black soldiers in the American Revolution is still largely buried in the graveyard of forgotten history.

Out of the millions of words written about the war, only a relative handful bother to acknowledge the contributions made by black soldiers at Lexington, Concord, Bunker Hill, Fort Ticonderoga, Saratoga, Yorktown, and all the other battlefields where black men suffered and died alongside white men to create this nation.

It is as if those black patriots never existed and yet, without them, the war for independence from Great Britain might have been lost.

When we think of soldiers suffering through the hunger, disease, and cold at Valley Forge, we do not think of black men like Phillip Field. Yet he was there.

When we think of Ethan Allen and his Green Mountain Boys capturing Fort Ticonderoga "in the name of the Great Jehovah and the Continental Congress," we do not think of black Green Mountain Boys like Lemuel Haynes or Barzillai Lew storming those stone walls. Yet they were there.

When we picture brave patriots massing at Lexington and Concord in 1775 to defy the British Redcoats, we do not think of black men as being part of that bold group. Yet Cuff Whitemore, Peter Salem, and almost a dozen other black patriots stood side by side with white ones when the course of history was changed forever by "the shot heard round the world."

From Lexington and Concord at the beginning of

the war, to the surrender of the British army at Yorktown that sealed the outcome of that brutal struggle, black soldiers sacrificed their lives for freedom.

"It was not for their own land they fought, not even for a land which had adopted them, but for a land which had enslaved them, and whose laws, even in freedom, oftener oppressed than protected," novelist Harriet Beecher Stowe (*Uncle Tom's Cabin*) wrote in 1855 in the introduction to William Cooper Nell's book, *The Colored Patriots of the American Revolution.* "Bravery, under such circumstances, has a peculiar beauty and merit."

There were almost one million men of fighting age in the colonies when the war began, but George Washington's Continental Army never numbered more than 30,000 during the seven years of the war. Many people did not care which side won and others were opposed to the war for independence. Some experts have estimated that at the beginning of the Revolutionary War, as few as one third of the population was willing to fight for freedom from Great Britain.

When Washington and his battered army went into winter quarters at Valley Forge, Pennsylvania, in that desperate winter of 1777–78, he had just 9,000 men. By March, more than 3,000 had deserted, and the cause of freedom hung by a thread.

Another 3,000 of his troops were confined to

hospitals or nearby farmers' houses, declared Washington in a letter to the President of the Continental Congress (Henry Laurens of South Carolina), "for want of shoes," while almost 2,000 were without blankets and were "obliged . . . to sit up all night by fires, instead of taking comfortable rest in the natural and common way. . . ."

Conditions were so bad that there was a mutiny which, Washington reported, "with difficulty was suppressed by the spirited exertions of some officers. . . ."

It was becoming increasingly hard to find men willing to fight in a war already known for its brutality. By the time the Revolutionary War was over, 0.9 percent of the country's population of almost three million would be killed (in the history of this country's wars, this percentage of the population killed is second only to that of the Civil War).

Into the midst of this dark night of America's hope for freedom, 5,000 black men came to the Continental Army, enlisted in the cause and — unlike most white soldiers who served short terms in state militias — served throughout the war in the force that bore the brunt of the fighting.

While many other people in revolutionary America talked of freedom as a political ideal while practicing slavery (like George Washington, Thomas Jefferson, John Paul Jones, Patrick Henry, and Paul Revere), these black soldiers were totally committed to the reality of freedom for themselves and everyone else.

Their spirit is perhaps best exemplified by Lemuel Haynes, who proudly proclaimed, 40 years after the Revolutionary War was over, that he had once "devoted all for the sake of freedom and independence, and endured frequent campaigns in their defence, and has never viewed the sacrifice as too great.

"And should an attack be made on this sacred ark [the United States]," declared the eighty-year-old Haynes, "the poor remains of life would be devoted to its defence."

This book is an attempt to tell the story of Lemuel Haynes and the thousands of other brave black men who watered the soil of freedom with their blood, helping to bring about the birth of a nation we now call the United States of America.

It is one of the most remarkable and moving stories in American history, and one we all must know if we are to understand ourselves and the heritage we share.

CHAPTER

I

The night of March 5, 1770, was clear and cold, and the young moon that rose over Beacon Hill revealed a thin film of ice on the snow that covered the ground. There were few people on the narrow, unlit streets, but that would quickly change.

Tensions had been rising all winter between the citizens of Boston and British soldiers stationed in the city of 16,000. The soldiers were not only an occupying army, but also competed for jobs at a time when jobs were scarce throughout the colonies.

Violence sparked by the anger of those with little money, power, or property was nothing new in colonial America. It had been part of life in the colonies since at least 1676, when black slaves, white indentured servants, and small white landowners joined forces in an unsuccessful attempt to overthrow the government of Virginia.

Before their uprising was put down, they burned the

capital at Jamestown, chased the governor out of town, and forced England to send 1,000 soldiers across the Atlantic to restore order.

Since that time there had been 17 other uprisings aimed at overthrowing colonial governments, 6 black rebellions against slavery, and 40 riots by poor farmers, laborers, and others infuriated by the poverty they endured while rich merchants and large landowners prospered.

By 1770, Boston was the site of much of this anger. Just five percent of the population owned almost half the town's wealth. Laborers and others on the bottom rung of the economic ladder found it increasingly hard to make ends meet.

Their struggle was made even harder by the competition from the poorly-paid British soldiers. As a result, there were bloody brawls throughout the winter of 1769–70 between British soldiers and colonial workers.

Boston was now like a powder keg waiting for one spark to make it explode, and that spark came on the night of March 5.

At about nine o'clock, reported the *Boston Gazette*, "some young lads" got into a scuffle with soldiers, resulting in a slight sword wound to one of the boys, and "presently 10 or 12 Soldiers came from the Barracks with their Cutlasses drawn."

Seeing the soldiers flourishing their swords, several

civilians "ran and set the Bells a ringing: This collected the People, who at length made the Soldiers retire to their Barracks. . . ."

Some of the people then made their way to the customhouse on King Street, where they threw snowballs and chunks of ice at the lone sentinel on duty. He loaded his gun, backed up the steps, and cried for help.

Captain Thomas Preston rushed out with eight soldiers, who formed into a half circle and "loaded and pointed their Guns breast-high to the People. . . ."

A slave named Andrew said there then "came down a number from Jackson's corner, huzzaing and crying, damn them, they dare not fire, we are not afraid of them."

A tall, sturdy seaman named Crispus Attucks quickly made his way to the front of the crowd. He was a part-black, part-Natick Indian who had escaped from slavery in nearby Framingham 20 years before (in the Natick language, *attuck* means "deer"). Attucks could not have known that as he hurried from his supper in answer to the tolling of the fire bells, he was also hurrying into history.

Armed "with a long cordwood stick," according to Andrew, Attucks "threw himself in, and made a blow at the officer. . . ."

And then, as the bells continued to sound throughout the wakening town and men shouted and cursed, the soldiers fired. Attucks was the first to die, pitching forward into the gutter with two musket balls in his chest.

By the time the firing ceased and the smoke cleared in what quickly became known throughout the colonies as the Boston Massacre, the blood of four other dead and dying men stained the snow.

In addition to Attucks, there was Patrick Carr, an Irish-born journeyman leathermaker; Samuel Gray, a ropemaker; James Caldwell, a ship's mate; and Samuel Maverick, apprentice to an ivory turner.

"On that night," future president John Adams wrote many years later, "the foundation of American independence was laid."

Just a few days after the killings, however, in his role as defense lawyer for the soldiers, he spoke derisively of the dead men as "a rabble of negroes, &c."

Adams was especially scornful of Attucks, "to whose mad behavior, in all probability, the dreadful carnage of that night is chiefly ascribed."

Most colonists saw the victims as martyrs to the cause of independence from Britain, however, and the largest funeral procession ever assembled in North America followed their bodies to the Middle Burying Ground.

Over a hundred years later, when a handsome monument was erected over the vault where they lay, poet John Boyle O'Reilly wrote that Attucks was "The first to defy, and the first to die, with Maverick, Carr, and Gray. . . ."

It could hardly have been more ironic that the first blood shed to help lay the foundation for American independence was that of a fugitive slave who could still be returned to slavery under the laws of Massachusetts and every other colony.

In 1770, over 400,000 African Americans were held in slavery in a total population of a little over 2.1 million (there were also several thousand Native American slaves).

Many white colonists recognized the hypocrisy of demanding liberty from Britain for themselves while holding hundreds of thousands of men, women, and children in slavery because of the color of their skin.

"Does it follow that it is right to enslave a man because he is black?" Boston lawyer and Patriot leader James Otis asked his fellow colonists. "Will short curled hair, like wool . . . help the argument? Can any logical inference in favour of slavery be drawn from a flat nose, a long or short face?"

But although antislavery pamphlets began to be published with increasing frequency, the majority of colonists continued to support slavery.

Just three weeks after the Boston Massacre, master silversmith and engraver Paul Revere issued a print of the scene. There was no sign of Crispus Attucks in the scene. Instead, in the print that was to become the official Patriot version of the incident, Revere portrayed an all-white crowd defying the British soldiers.

Colonial resistance to British rule largely collapsed in the months following the killings of Attucks and the others, thanks to Britain's repeal of four of the five unpopular tax laws (only the one on tea remained), withdrawal of British troops to Castle Island in Boston Harbor, and a gradual return to prosperity.

But the words about freedom and liberty had stirred the hopes of those colonists who enjoyed the least freedom and liberty: blacks, women, laborers, white indentured servants, and the many small farmers struggling to survive against the oppression of wealthy landowners.

In the disputed territory claimed by both New York and New Hampshire (present-day Vermont), a huge frontiersman named Ethan Allen led the struggle against the large landowners.

He and his followers — who included black men as well as white — sought relief in the courts. But when a judge in Albany, New York, ruled against them, Allen rose in the back of the courtroom and cried defiantly: "The gods of the valleys are not the gods of the hills."

He then led his illegal army, the Green Mountain Boys, in guerrilla warfare against the landowners.

But no single group had more reason to rebel during this tumultuous time, or was more feared by colonial rulers and the public, than African Americans.

There were free black people in every colony, but the vast majority were held in slavery. There had been slave revolts throughout the history of the colonies, and the fear of such revolts was ever present, especially in the South with its large slave population.

With the American Revolution drawing ever closer and talk of freedom all around them, African Americans seemed more determined than ever to make freedom a reality for themselves and their children.

On April 20, 1773, Peter Bestes, Chester Joie, Sambo Freeman, and Felix Holbrok — four slaves seeking freedom for themselves, their wives, and their children — wrote a letter to delegates in the Massachusetts House of Representatives that began almost tauntingly: "The efforts made by the legislative of this province in their last sessions to free themselves from slavery, gave us, who are in that deplorable state, a high degree of satisfaction. We expect great things from men who have made such a noble stand against the designs of their *fellow-men* to enslave them. . . ."

The delegates refused to consider the petition and when the four men appealed to Governor Thomas Hutchinson, he also rejected them.

Other slaves turned to violence to try to gain their

freedom, even though the penalties for slave revolts could be barbaric.

In December 1774, after the capture of several slaves in Georgia who had killed an overseer and three other whites, two of the slaves were burned alive by authorities.

In Virginia, responding to another slave conspiracy, future president and Revolutionary War leader James Madison cautioned his fellow slaveholders that "it is prudent such things should be concealed as well as suppressed," lest the news encourage other slaves to fight for freedom.

A conspiracy was even discovered in Boston, according to John Adams's wife, Abigail, who told him about it and then added: "I wish most sincerely, there was not a slave in the province; it always appeared a most iniquitous scheme to me to fight ourselves for what we are daily robbing and plundering from those who have as good a right to freedom as we have."

Poor whites, especially indentured servants who were often treated as harshly as black slaves, were also deeply stirred by the widespread talk of liberty and freedom.

Many wealthy planters, including George Washington, bought slaves (whom they owned for life) and indentured servants (whom they owned for a specific number of years). They advertised for the indentured servants when they ran away and punished them with flogging, branding, and additional years of servitude when they were recaptured.

In Philadelphia, an astonished Englishman wrote home to his father, "They sell the [white] servants here as they do their horses, and advertise them as they do their beef and oatmeal."

The indentured servants often worked alongside black slaves in fields and shops, developed close relationships with them, and sometimes joined them in conspiracies to run away or fight for freedom.

On the eve of the American Revolution, however, the struggle for freedom by most poor people — especially blacks, who were increasingly watched by armed patrols — was a struggle undertaken by individuals acting alone or with a few friends.

But that would quickly change.

The Massachusetts villages of Lexington and Concord were quiet, peaceful places where several black people lived among the predominantly white population. The majority were slaves, although some were free. In common with their white neighbors, most worked on farms.

Among these African Americans were David Lamson, a veteran of the French and Indian War; Lemuel Haynes, a twenty-one-year-old who loved to read and who would one day receive the first honorary degree of

Master of Arts bestowed on an African American; and Peter Salem, soon to rise from obscurity to fame.

All must have been as aware as their fellow farmers and villagers of the rising tensions between the British and the colonists. No one was more effective at exploiting those tensions in order to further the cause of colonial independence than a man called the Great Agitator and, later, Father of American Independence: Samuel Adams, cousin to John Adams.

For over a decade, while Thomas Jefferson, George Washington, Benjamin Franklin, and most other leaders tried to find ways to maintain the colonists' ties with the British, Samuel Adams worked feverishly to sever those ties.

When Adams wanted a demonstration, he would get in touch with his friend, Paul Revere, who knew many laborers and artisans, and Revere would see to it there was a demonstration.

Another friend of Adams's was Boston's leading merchant, a young man named John Hancock. Hancock had inherited a large fortune, and quickly made it larger by becoming one of the biggest smugglers in the colonies.

By the time the Revolutionary War began in 1775, British authorities had brought almost 500 indictments against Hancock for smuggling tea and other items.

The survival of his smuggling operation was threatened in 1773, however, when the British granted the East India Company the right to sell unlimited amounts of tea in the colonies at rock-bottom prices.

Samuel Adams sent Revere and other couriers riding throughout New England, warning that the low-priced tea was simply a British tactic to gain control over all goods imported into the colonies. Once they achieved that goal, Adams declared, the British would then control the colonists' lives more firmly than ever.

On December 16, 1773, at the end of an angry public meeting called by Adams, crowds poured into the streets, shouting, "Boston harbor a teapot tonight!"

Men, disguised as Mohawk Indians, rushed to Griffin's Wharf, boarded three British ships loaded with tea, hoisted all 340 chests from the holds, and scattered their contents in Boston Harbor.

Adams, eager for the struggle against the British to begin, sent Paul Revere galloping off to New York and Philadelphia to spread the news about the Boston "Tea Party." Many wealthy colonists, including John Adams and George Washington, denounced this destruction of private property as mob violence.

Other men of wealth also feared the growing involvement of common people in actions that could profoundly effect the economic and political life of the colonies, which the wealthy had always controlled.

Thomas Jefferson, reflecting this view, called city

workingmen "the swinish multitude," and "the panders of vice and the instruments by which the liberties of a country are generally overthrown."

When word of the Tea Party reached England, the British government moved swiftly to crush the Boston "rebellion" and punish the town. Under a series of laws called the Coercive Acts, Britain closed Boston's port, prohibited town meetings, and sent more soldiers to serve as an army of occupation.

One of the acts authorized the British army to seize any buildings it wanted, including private homes, and to station armed soldiers anywhere among the civilian population. This act applied to all the colonies.

By August 1774, seven British regiments under the command of General Thomas Gage were stationed in Boston. Towns throughout New England began to store powder and cannon for the war with England that now seemed inevitable.

During that same month, George Washington told a friend that "the crisis is arrived when we must assert our rights, or submit to every imposition, that can be heaped upon us, till custom and use shall make us as tame and abject slaves, as the blacks we rule over with such arbitrary sway."

The colonists' growing defiance of the British government was quickly bringing them, John Adams wrote Jefferson, to the "edge of the precipice."

And it was a dangerous precipice, with the possibility of a horrible death at the end of it. The penalty for treason recently handed down by an English judge against Irish patriots who rebelled against British rule, proved just how horrible that death could be.

The Irish patriots were ordered to be hanged by the neck, but not until dead. Instead, the judge declared, the still living bodies "are to be taken down, your bowels torn out and burned before your faces, your head then cut off, and your bodies divided into four quarters . . . and may the Almighty God have Mercy on your souls."

Delegates from all of the colonies but Georgia, attended a meeting of the First Continental Congress in Philadelphia from September 5 to October 26, 1774, and advised Massachusetts to declare independence. They also urged every colony to form militias. Militia members who were ready to march or fight at a minute's notice were called Minutemen.

Throughout the winter, Massachusetts colonists prepared for war.

On April 14, 1775, General Gage received a secret document ordering him to use force to end the rebellion and arrest its "principal actors and abettors."

He sent two spies to map out the countryside, a Colonel Smith and a man named John Howe. They stopped at a tavern and were waited on by a black woman who had lived in Boston and knew many of the British officers and soldiers by sight.

Howe later said that when Colonel Smith asked where the two of them could find employment, "she looked Col. Smith in the face, and said, Smith you will find employment enough for you and all Gen. Gage's men in a few months." Smith appeared "to be thunder-struck" that she knew who he was, and told Howe he would kill the woman if he came back that way with his regiment.

At last Gage was ready to act. Shortly after 2 A.M. on the morning of April 19, a column of 700 British officers and men began to march into a cold west wind. Their destination was Concord, which was twenty miles away, five miles beyond the village of Lexington.

At Concord they planned to "seize and destroy all Artillery, Ammunition, Provisions, Tents, Small Arms, and all Military Stores whatever." Leaders of the expedition were also under orders to arrest John Hancock and Samuel Adams, so the two could be taken to England and tried as rebels.

But unknown to the commander, Lieutenant Colonel Francis Smith, and his second in command, Major John Pitcairn, word of their "secret" expedition was already being spread to thousands of patriots.

The soldiers had left their barracks about 10 P.M.,

and an hour later Paul Revere was racing toward Lexington on a swift borrowed horse named Brown Beauty. Other couriers were also riding hard, including one who was alerted when Revere lit two signal lamps in the steeple of Boston's Old North Church.

"The Regulars are coming out!" the couriers cried as they rode through the sleeping countryside, and by 3 A.M., the alarm had spread as far as Tewksbury, 25 miles north of Boston.

In every town, the couriers gave each individual commander the news. And in town after town, Minutemen awoke, armed themselves, and headed for Lexington and Concord.

Revere found Hancock and Adams hiding in the Lexington house of Captain John Parker, and the two were soon on their way. Parker, the town's militia leader, roused his drummer boy and the two hurried to the village green, where the youth beat a loud call to arms that sent the Minutemen scrambling for their weapons.

Down in Virginia, Patrick Henry had recently warned his colleagues that war between the colonies and England could break out at any hour.

"Is life so dear, or peace so sweet as to be purchased at the price of chains and slavery?" he asked. "Forbid it, Almighty God! I know not what course others may take, but as for me, give me liberty or give me death!"

The slave-owning Patrick Henry intended his words to apply only to white Americans, but in Lexington and Concord, African Americans were preparing to fight for freedom alongside their white neighbors.

The sun was just rising when British soldiers came charging toward Lexington Green, more than a dozen companies on foot with mounted soldiers pounding along on either side of them.

The free Lemuel Haynes and a slave named Prince Easterbrooks had grabbed their weapons and raced to the Green at the sound of the drumroll. Now they stood in Captain Parker's company with the rest of the Minutemen, watching anxiously as the British suddenly quickened their speed.

There seemed to be about 1,000 troops, said John Robbins, another member of Parker's company, "huzzaing, and on a quick pace towards us, with three officers . . . on full gallop toward us, the foremost of which cried, 'Throw down your arms, ye villains, ye rebels. . . .'"

The Minutemen held onto their weapons, but began to disperse. And then a shot rang out. Which side fired it is still not known, but "the shot heard round the world" would change the course of history.

Soon thousands of armed farmers would come swarming down, eager to do battle with the British trying desperately to fight their way back to Boston.

"What a glorious morning is this!" cried a jubilant Samuel Adams when he learned of the fighting.

The Revolutionary War, that "most trying and terrific struggle" he had worked for for so long, had begun at last.

CHAPTER
2

British officers tried desperately to control their men after the first shot rang out on Lexington Green, but the soldiers were an angry mob raging out of control. British Lieutenant Colonel Francis Smith, who came riding up after the shot was fired, said the scene looked like the end of the world with six companies of infantrymen firing in all directions.

"The men were so wild, they could hear no orders," remembered another English officer, Lieutenant John Barker.

Other companies, drawn by the sound of the firing, surged through Lexington, shooting and stabbing militiamen wherever they found them. Many stopped fighting to loot houses.

By the time Smith restored some semblance of order, eight Patriots lay dead, including one who crawled to his house on the edge of the green and died in the arms of his family. Another nine were wounded.

Smith ordered his officers to proceed to Concord and complete the expedition, even though the countryside would now be alive with armed farmers rushing to the scene.

His officers protested, saying such a move would be suicidal and that it was imperative they start for Boston right away. But Smith replied: "I have my orders. I am determined to obey them."

The British made their way unmolested to Concord, though more and more men gathered to watch them from the surrounding hills. In Concord the soldiers destroyed the arms and materiel they found hidden in almost two dozen farms and homes, then prepared to leave the town.

Minutemen and militia units were now rushing toward Lexington, Concord, and the road to Boston from settlements throughout the area. Some of the black men hurrying to the fighting were Peter Salem of Framingham; Isaiah Bayoman and Job Potama of Stoneham; Pompy of Braintree; Cato Stedman, Cuff Whitemore ("Cuff" or "Cuffee" was a name commonly given black men during this period), and Cato Boardman of Cambridge; Pomp Blackman whose town is unknown, but who would go on to fight in the Continental Army; and Samuel Craft of Newton.

While the main British force was in Concord, a column of about 400 Patriots marched on the North

Bridge outside of Concord. The bridge was guarded by approximately 100 British soldiers.

As the Americans neared the bridge, someone fired a shot. As at Lexington, no one knows which side the shot came from, but within seconds everyone was shooting. Four of the eight British officers on the bridge were hit, along with one sergeant and six privates.

Three of the colonists had been killed and several wounded, but their comrades kept up such a withering fire the soldiers fled "despite all that could be done to prevent them," declared one of their officers.

Finally Colonel Smith led his men out of Concord, joined the column with other companies he had sent out to search for more hidden arms, and began the march back toward Boston.

The Americans followed him closely, firing at his column from behind the stone fences and trees that lined the road. Sometimes they fought from houses near the road, constantly harassing the British who were slowed down by the buggies and wagons carrying their wounded.

Units from the various towns were now beginning to coordinate their attacks. By mid-afternoon 2,000 attacked the British from behind and from the sides, while another 2,000 waited farther down the road to Boston.

Even men who were exempt from military duty because of their age joined in the fight.

Near West Cambridge, 12 old men turned out and "chose for their leader David Lamson, a mulatto, who had served in the [French and Indian] war. . . . They took their position . . . behind a bank wall of earth and stones."

Lamson was of mixed black and white parentage, but the term "mulatto" was also used in colonial times to describe people of mixed Native American and white parentage, or of mixed Native American and black parentage.

When the British troops drew near, Lamson "ordered his men to rise and aim directly at the horses, and called out to them to surrender. No reply was made, but the drivers whipped up their teams. Lamson's men then fired, killing several of the horses and two of the men and wounding others."

The courage of Lamson and his men resulted in the capture of part of the British supply team and its military escort.

The British retreat was now a rout which the officers tried to stop by threatening to kill their men with bayonets.

Lord Hugh Percy, commander of the British reinforcements, said many of the Patriots "concealed themselves in houses, & advanced within 10 yds. to fire at me & other officers, tho' they were morally certain of being put to death themselves in an instant."

British soldiers enraged at being shot at from houses, broke into several homes and killed everyone inside, then burned the buildings.

And still the Patriots came on. Now 3,000 strong, they attacked the rear of the column, taunted the soldiers to stand and fight, and constantly shouted, "Hancock! Hancock! Hancock forever!"

With the sun going down in a fiery sky, the British finally pushed across the narrow Charlestown Neck and onto the slopes of Bunker's Hill and Breed's Hill, the highest points in Charlestown.

There they began digging in under the protective guns of the British navy's sixty-four-gun man-of-war, *Somerset.*

The last colonial casualty, according to British Captain Fredrick Mackenzie, was a black man who "was wounded near the houses close to the Neck, out of which the Rebels fired to the last."

By the time the day was over, the British had 70 dead, 182 wounded, and 22 missing. The Patriot losses were 49 dead, 39 wounded, and 5 missing from almost two dozen towns. One of the casualties on the "List of the Names of the Provincials who were Killed and Wounded," was Prince Easterbrooks of Lexington, "a Negro man."

Before the clashes at Lexington and Concord, many of the colonies' leaders still clung to the hope that their differences with England could be settled without war, but now those hopes were gone.

"No man was a warmer wisher for reconciliation than myself before the fatal nineteenth of April, 1775," wrote Thomas Paine, a working-class English immigrant whose essays on freedom would soon rally tens of thousands to the cause of American independence, "but the moment the event of that day was known, I rejected the hardened, sullen-tempered Pharaoh of England forever."

News of the clashes spread like wildfire, thanks in part to the propaganda efforts of Samuel Adams ("Women in childbed were driven by the soldiery naked into the streets, old men peaceably in their houses were shot dead," read a pamphlet almost certainly written by Adams and distributed by Dr. Joseph Warren).

Eager volunteers flocked to Boston from throughout New England and other Northern colonies to enlist in the new army under the temporary command of General Artemas Ward, and the rebel army laying siege to the British at Boston quickly swelled to 15,000. Only one regiment came from the South, however, a Virginia unit commanded by Colonel Daniel Morgan.

Samuel Adams and John Hancock hurried to Philadelphia to join other delegates to the Second

Continental Congress, convened on May 10, 1775, to coordinate the rebellion against England.

Adams and Hancock, along with several other leaders from New England, were greeted like conquering heroes all along the route. In Philadelphia, said one observer, "all the bells were set to ringing and chiming, and every mark of respect that could be was expressed; not much, I presume, to the secret liking of their fellow delegates from the other colonies. . . ."

Despite the blood that had now been shed, many delegates to the Congress still hesitated to make a final break with England.

Just one month before, Benjamin Franklin had told an English friend that he knew of no American, "drunk or sober," who wanted independence from England.

Now even Thomas Jefferson drew back before the fateful step of declaring independence, and for once Samuel Adams also hesitated.

Then one morning, before that day's congressional session began, John Adams told Samuel that he was "determined to take a step which should compel all the members of Congress to declare themselves for or against something. I am determined this morning to make a direct motion that Congress should adopt the army before Boston, and appoint Colonel Washington commander of it."

Washington had not come right out and asked for

the appointment, but he made his wishes known by wearing his nearly twenty-year-old French and Indian War uniform to every session of congress. The struggle against the British was still largely being waged by New England, and John Adams felt that placing a Southerner in command of the army would bring the Southern colonies into the conflict.

After a two-day debate, George Washington was named commander in chief of the army laying siege to Boston: henceforth to be known as the Continental Army.

With all-out war growing ever closer, Ethan Allen saw a chance to advance the cause of his small farmers against the landowners by joining the fight against the British.

On May 10, 1775 — the same day Washington was appointed commander in chief — Allen and Benedict Arnold quietly led more than 80 Green Mountain Boys across Lake Champlain toward the mighty stone walls of Fort Ticonderoga.

The British-held fort was called "the key to North America," controlling access from Canada in the north to the Hudson River valley in the south.

"You that will undertake, poise your firelocks," Allen said, and each man — indicating his readiness to follow their eager leader — prepared his gun for firing.

Allen and Arnold then led a charge through a small gate, with the men crying, "No quarter! No quarter!"

Among those charging into the fort with their fellow Vermonters were Lemuel Haynes and at least three other African-American Green Mountain Boys: Primus Black, Epheram Blackman, and Barzillai Lew, a veteran of the French and Indian War described as "a giant."

An astonished British lieutenant wearing only a red coat and holding his breeches in his hands, nervously poked his head through a door, staring wide-eyed at the huge leader and his men.

"Come out of there, you damned old rat!" Allen yelled.

When the officer asked by what authority he had invaded a British fort, Allen is said to have waved his sword at the man's head and shouted: "In the name of the Great Jehovah and the Continental Congress!"

He then threatened to massacre everyone in the fort unless "the Fort and the effects of George the Third" were handed over immediately. The keys to the fort were quickly handed over, along with ninety gallons of rum (which were quickly opened), and over two hundred cannons, howitzers, and mortars. Over half the captured artillery was in usable or repairable condition, and would prove priceless to the Continental Army.

In Boston, the British were reinforcing their garrison and had sent over three major generals on the warship, *Cerberus:* John Burgoyne, William Howe, and Henry Clinton.

"I don't know what the Americans will think of them," said Lord North, the king's adviser. "But I know that they make me tremble."

They did not make the Americans tremble, however. In fact, the colonists taunted the generals with the following rhyme:

> Behold the *Cerberus* the Atlantic plow
> Her precious cargo, Burgoyne, Clinton, Howe.
> Bow, wow, wow!

But the 5,000 troops the British now had in Boston were no laughing matter. Gage had ordered his men to abandon Bunker's Hill and Breed's Hill in late April, but after the arrival of Burgoyne, Clinton, and Howe, the four made plans to retake that high ground.

The Patriots learned of the British plans and moved swiftly. On the night of June 16, nearly 1,000 of them under the command of Colonel William Prescott, crept onto Breed's Hill and began furiously building fortifications near the top. Their leaders had decided that Breed's Hill could be more easily defended than the higher Bunker's Hill, which was directly exposed to the guns of the British warships.

The sound of pickaxes and spades clanging against rocks could be heard in Boston and Charlestown. Clinton warned his fellow generals that the British forces should be ready to attack the hill at dawn, but they ignored him and went to bed.

Sampson Talbert of Bridgewater, one of the black Patriots working on Breed's Hill, said it was the "hottest day's work he had ever done." A Charlestown resident who heard the sounds declared that the men "careed it on with the utmost viger all night."

When daylight came, the men were still at it, trying to complete a redoubt made of earth and stone, with walls 6 feet high. The angled walls in front came to a point and were almost 150 feet long. The amount they had accomplished in one night was amazing, and the British reaction was swift and violent.

Within minutes more than 100 big warship guns began firing at the redoubt. A cannonball took off the head of one militiaman who started down the hill for water, leading some of the others to desert.

Prescott drew his sword and leaped onto the wall. While cannonballs fell all around him, he walked back and forth trying to rally his troops by shouting, "It was a one in a million shot, men!"

Future president John Quincy Adams was one of the thousands of civilians who saw the fighting. Years later he recalled how, as a child, he stood with his mother and heard "the thundering cannon" and saw "the smoke of burning Charlestown . . . on that awful day. . . ."

The exhausted Americans worked feverishly to complete the redoubt, and finally finished in the early afternoon. They also built a breastwork — a wall that ran partway down one side of the hill to protect their flanks. The work was completed just in time.

General Howe crossed over from Boston with a fleet of 28 barges filled with 1,500 of his finest soldiers, and they began their slow march up the hill to the accompaniment of fifes and drums.

There were 3,500 militia and Minutemen on the hill by now, though one American said they consisted of "raw lads and old men half armed, with no practice in discipline, commanded without order, and God knows by whom."

Nineteen-year-old Private Simon Fobes of Bridgewater said he was shocked when the battle began to see that "my fellow-soldiers were running at full speed down the hill" and "my officers [were] dodging first one way, then the other. . . ."

Patriot Captain John Chester said he had to threaten to shoot an officer and the men he was leading before they would go back up the hill.

But many of the veterans of Lexington and Concord were also there, along with Dr. Joseph Warren. He had just been named a general in the Massachusetts

Provincial Army and was also president of the Provincial Congress.

A friend said Warren once told him he wanted to die fighting the British "in blood up to his knees." Now he would have that chance.

The British soldiers were now nearing the redoubt, led by the biggest men in the British army, the Grenadiers. When they were just a few yards away, the colonials fired.

Lead balls, old nails, and jagged pieces of metal came blasting at the Grenadiers, melting their line with a burst of pain and blood. Dead men dotted the ground, and the wounded lay screaming.

Finally the first wave broke and ran under the galling fire. Some of the Redcoats made their way back down and into the barges, but their officers forced them out again with curses and swords.

By now, almost 2,000 British soldiers had been thrown into the battle, and the firing from their war-ships was joined by cannon that the soldiers were fi-nally able to drag up Breed's Hill and aim at the redoubt.

There were also clashes on other parts of the hill and on Bunker's Hill as well. Some of the black Patriots fighting there were Barzillai Lew, Peter Salem, and Salem Poor.

Other African Americans standing shoulder-to-shoulder with their white comrades and contesting every foot of the British advance were Alexander Ames, Charleston Eads, Sampson Talbert, Seymour Burr, Cuff Hayes, Pomp Fisk, Titus Coburn, Grant Cooper, Cuff Whitemore, and Jude Hall.

Hall, who had come down from New Hampshire, would fight so well during the battle that the other soldiers nicknamed him "Old Rock."

Major William Lawrence, who was wounded in the battle, said the black men he saw on the hill showed a "courage, military discipline, and fidelity" he would remember "with respect" for the rest of his life.

The twenty-two-year-old Caesar Brown, who had also fought at Lexington, cried: "Now, Caesar, give them some more!" as he fired his last shot at the British and then was killed.

Salem Poor, a free black man serving in Captain Benjamin Ames's militia company, fought so courageously he would be praised more than almost any other Patriot in what came to be called the Battle of Bunker Hill.

Some observers said his shooting brought down one of the senior British officers, Lieutenant Colonel James Abercrombie, as Abercrombie sprang onto the redoubt shouting: "Surrender, you rebels!"

The exhausted and enraged British soldiers, suddenly realizing the Patriots were out of ammunition, gave an angry shout that could be heard across the water in Boston. And then they charged the redoubt with fixed bayonets and vaulted onto the walls.

Among the Patriots still fighting there, giving some of their comrades time to escape, were Dr. Warren, Peter Salem, and Cuff Whitemore.

One of the last men to escape wrote his mother that he "Jump'd over the walls and ran half a mile, while balls flew like hailstones and cannon roared like thunder."

Peter Salem is generally credited with killing British Major John Pitcairn, though that isn't known for certain. Pitcairn, followed closely by his son and other troops, leaped onto the redoubt wall and shouted exultingly: "The day is ours!"

No sooner had Pitcairn cried out, said Samuel Swett, who wrote the earliest history of the battle, than "Salem, a black soldier, and a number of others, shot him through and he fell. . . ."

The "Peter Salem Gun" is now on display at the Bunker Hill Monument.

Salem and Poor managed to break their way out of the fort along with several others, but Dr. Warren was shot in the head while trying to follow. A Redcoat stood over him with bayonet poised, while the dying Warren asked to be spared further wounds.

Now that they had finally managed to reach the enemy that had taken such a heavy toll on them, the British soldiers went wild.

"Nothing could be more shocking than the carnage that followed the storming of this work," one of the British officers wrote. "We tumbled over the dead to get at the living who were crowding out of the redoubt."

Smoke, powder, and dust were so thick that one American could only escape by feeling his way out. All the while, the British soldiers slashed wildly with their bayonets. An officer later counted thirty Americans "killed by the bayonet" inside the redoubt.

The soldier standing above Dr. Warren cursed the pleading man and drove a bayonet through him, then looted the body of its silk-fringed waistcoat and breeches.

Captain Walter Laurie of the British burial detail said he "stuffed the scoundrel [Dr. Warren] with another Rebel into one hole and there he and his seditious principles may remain."

The Battle of Bunker Hill was over and it had cost the British almost half their men: more than 1,000 casualties out of 2,300 rank and file, including 226 killed and 828 wounded. The Patriot losses were 140 men killed, 271 wounded, and 30 taken prisoner.

All the casualties had occurred during about an hour and a half, and in a space less than one half mile square.

"I wish we could sell them another hill at the same

price," declared Nathanael Greene, one of the Patriot commanders.

"The loss we have Sustained is greater than we can bear," General Gage wrote back to England. *I wish this Cursed place was burned!*"

CHAPTER
3

Less than three weeks after the Battle of Bunker Hill, George Washington arrived in Cambridge to take command of the Continental Army.

With him was a young man named William Lee, one of the almost 200 slaves owned by Washington and his wife, Martha. Lee was bought by Washington seven years before and would be forced to accompany him throughout the war.

The young man must have been amazed to see African Americans in the colonial army. It was a crime punishable by a horrible death such as dismemberment or burning alive, for a black person to be caught carrying weapons in the South, where Lee had spent all his life.

The realization that there were so many black men in the army also must have made a strong impression on Washington and the few soldiers who had come from the South.

"Such Sermons, such Negroes, such Colonels, Such Boys and such Great Great Grandfathers," wrote one Southern soldier disparagingly of the army surrounding Boston.

Just one week after Washington arrived in Cambridge, his headquarters issued the following order to recruiting officers: "You are not to enlist any deserter from the Ministerial army, nor any stroller, negro, or vagabond, or person suspected of being an enemy to the liberty of America. . . ."

This order did not affect black men who were already in the army. There was increasing pressure from white Southerners to make the Continental Army all white, however, and many Northerners were sympathetic to such efforts.

Most Southern whites seemed to feel, as the earliest English settlers in the Carolinas once put it, that "there must be great caution used [in the military employment of Negroes] lest our slaves when armed might become our masters."

The same month Lemuel Haynes and other Patriots were fighting at Lexington and Concord, officials in several Southern colonies issued guns to put down any attempt by slaves to fight for their freedom.

At almost the same time the Battle of Bunker Hill was being waged, whites in North Carolina arrested dozens of slaves they feared were going to rise up and fight for their freedom.

"By night we had in custody and in goal near forty under proper guard . . . ," wrote the chairman of the Safety Committee in Chatham, North Carolina. "We posted guards upon the roads, for several miles that night."

The next day the Committee "ordered several to be severely whipt and sentenced several to receive 80 lashes each. . . ."

Even New York had a provision in its law requiring one third of the militiamen to stay home to guard against possible slave uprisings.

Knowing there could be no successful revolution unless North and South were united, John Adams expressed his concerns about using black soldiers to Brigadier General John Thomas, one of the New England militia commanders.

"We have some negroes," Thomas replied, ". . . and in action many of them have proved themselves brave. . . ."

Adams also questioned Brigadier General William Heath about black soldiers and Heath told him: "There are in the Massachusetts Regiments some negroes. Such is also the case with the Regiments from the Other Colonies, Rhode Island has a number of negroes and Indians, Connecticut has fewer negroes, but a number of Indians. The New Hampshire regiments have less of both."

On October 8, Washington called a council of war

of the nine generals in his command. Despite the hero- ism of the black soldiers at Lexington, Concord, and Bunker Hill, and despite the praise of many of their of- ficers, "It was agreed unanimously to reject all slaves; and, by a great majority, to reject negroes altogether."

Washington ordered that any black man found "straggling" near his headquarters, the army camps, or in nearby villages be seized and jailed. He also di- rected the quartermaster general to supply clothes to all those soldiers who wished to re-enlist, "Negroes ex- cepted."

Washington's feelings against arming black men must have been powerful, since he was willing to ban them at a time when the Continental Army was des- perate for men. Many soldiers had simply decided to go home after the Battle of Bunker Hill, and others were about to be discharged because their enlistments were up.

Although the Continental Congress had created the Army, the colonies only loaned their units for short pe- riods of time and could withdraw them whenever they wanted.

"In short," Washington wrote his adjutant general, Joseph Reed, near the end of November, "after the last of this month, our lines will be so weakened, that the minute-men and militia must be called in for their defence. . . ."

Washington, Adams, and the other leaders of the

Revolutionary War were now faced with the dilemma of how to wage a war for freedom while at the same time defending the practice of slavery.

"For shame," wrote New England clergyman Nathaniel Niles, "let us either cease to enslave our fellow-men, or else let us cease to complain of those that would enslave us."

Adding his voice to those of a growing chorus of antislavery writers was Thomas Paine, who not only condemned the hypocrisy of American slave owners, but warned that the slaves could become a dangerous force within the country "should any enemy promise them a better condition."

Though the Patriots did not yet know it, General Gage had already written to Lord Barrington: "Things are now come to that crisis, that we must avail ourselves of every resource, even to raise the Negroes, in our cause."

A worried John Adams confided to his diary the "melancholy" news brought by two visitors, one from Georgia and the other from South Carolina.

They told him "that if one thousand regular (British) troops should land in Georgia, and their commander be provided with arms and clothes enough, and proclaim freedom to all the negroes who would join his camp, twenty thousand negroes would join it from the two Provinces in a fortnight."

Lemuel Haynes, Peter Salem, Sampson Talbert, and

the other black veterans had protested bitterly at the decision to exclude them from the army. Washington refused to change his mind, however, until the danger Thomas Paine had warned about seemed ready to happen.

In November 1775, from aboard the warship HMS *William* in the harbor at Norfolk, Virginia, British Governor Lord Dunmore issued a proclamation giving freedom to all "indented servants [whom he said were 'little better than white slaves'], Negroes, or others, (appertaining to Rebels) . . . that are able and willing to bear arms, they joining His Majesty's Troops, as soon as may be. . . ."

"The colonists," wrote one man, "were struck with horror" at Dunmore's proclamation.

Patrick Henry denounced the proclamation as "fatal to the publick Safety," and urged that slaves be guarded by "Constant, and well directed Patrols. . . ."

A Southern slave owner called for authorities to smash the slaves' "high notions of liberty" and "keep those mistaken creatures in awe."

Henry Laurens, a South Carolina slave owner who would soon be elected president of the Second Continental Congress, advised officials "to seize & if nothing else will do to destroy all those Rebellious slaves," even though he thought such an action would be "an awful business."

Some of the boldest slaves were willing to defy all the dangers and threats, however. One of these was a native of Africa named Thomas Peters. A descendant of a royal family of the Yoruba tribe described as "strong, far beyond the ordinary man," Peters was one of the first to run away and join the British.

Another was a slave named Charles who ran away one week after Dunmore's proclamation, complained his owner, because of a "determined resolution to get liberty, as he conceived it, by flying to Lord Dunmore."

Washington immediately recognized the threat Dunmore's offer posed to the American cause, especially in areas with large numbers of slaves. In Virginia, for instance, blacks greatly outnumbered whites and could swing the balance of power to the British if enough ran away.

"If the Virginians are wise," an alarmed Washington wrote Continental Congress member Richard Henry Lee, "that arch-traitor to the rights of humanity, Lord Dunmore, should be instantly crushed . . . that which renders the measure indispensably necessary is the negroes. For if he gets formidable, numbers will be tempted to join, who will be afraid to do it without."

Washington wasted no time in reversing his policy and letting the black veterans stay in the army.

Writing to John Hancock, the president of Congress, he said that "the free negroes who have served in this army are very much dissatisfied at being discarded. As it is to be apprehended that they may seek employment in the Ministerial [British] Army, I have . . . given license for their being enlisted."

Hundreds of black men had already made their way to Dunmore, despite increased slave patrols. And Dunmore was arming them "as fast as they came in," outfitting them in uniforms with the words "Liberty to Slaves" emblazoned across their chests.

Together with British soldiers and white indentured servants who had also escaped, they helped rout the colonial militia in a skirmish at Kemp's Landing near Norfolk, Virginia. One of the militia's commanders was chased into a swamp and captured by his own slave, who had recently escaped to the British.

Virginia had dispatched 1,000 militiamen to attack Dunmore and shut off the slaves' escape route from the interior to the sea. The Virginians and the British met at the Great Bridge south of Norfolk.

Unknown to the British, the Americans had prepared a heavily fortified breastworks on their side of the bridge, and the courage of a free black man gave them time to retreat to it.

The commander of the Second Virginia Regiment reported later that the man, William Flora, "was the last sentinel that came into the breast work. . . . He did not leave his post until he had fired several times. Billy had to cross a plank to get to the breast work, and had fairly passed over it when he was seen to turn back, and deliberately take up the plank after him, amidst a shower of musket balls. He . . . fired eight times."

The Americans inflicted heavy casualties on the British and forced them to retreat. The Battle of Great Bridge, which has been called the Lexington of the South, effectively ended Dunmore's chances of rallying large numbers of slaves to him by cutting off their main avenue of escape.

Flora would go on to serve in the Continental Army throughout the war, as would thousands of other black men, both slave and free. But as 1776 began, Washington and other leaders continued to agonize over the extent to which they could arm black men without threatening the institution of slavery.

Massachusetts passed an act in January barring "Indians, Negroes and Mulattoes" from serving in the state militia, an example that was quickly followed by the rest of New England.

In April, when New Hampshire asked all males above the age of twenty-one to sign a declaration promising to fight the British, the state excluded "lunatics, idiots, and Negroes."

New York, Pennsylvania, New Jersey, and Delaware quickly followed the lead of the New England colonies, usually also banning white indentured servants and Native Americans from bearing arms.

New Jersey even required black people to turn in whatever weapons they had "until the present troubles are settled."

Throughout the year, however, black men continued to join the ranks of the Continental Army for the simple reason that Washington and his officers needed them. Whites preferred to serve in their local militias where they could enlist for periods as short as one month and stay close to home.

And so, while African Americans were barred from most local and state militia units, they were increasingly accepted in the Continental Army.

On the night of March 4, 1776, following a plan devised by Washington and his generals, a vanguard of 800 men quietly made their way up Dorchester Heights, which overlooked Boston and the British warships in the harbor. To cover any noise the men might make, American artillery in Cambridge and Roxbury kept up a constant fire.

Among the African Americans in the vanguard were Primus Hall, David Lamson, and James Easton. They and the rest of the men made their way up the hill, said Washington, under a moon "shining in its full luster." A haze near the bottom of the Heights, however, shielded them from the sight of British sentries.

These first men were quickly followed by 1,200 more. Some carried picks and shovels, while others hauled over 300 carts filled with bales of hay, tree limbs, barrels of stones and sand, and prebuilt wooden gun platforms.

They worked feverishly all night and when dawn arrived, the British in Boston looked up to see fortifications bristling with guns looking down on them. The guns had been hauled on ox-drawn sledges from Fort Ticonderoga 200 miles away, through frozen forests and up and down countless snow-covered hills.

One awed British officer said the Americans must have had help from the "genie belonging to Alladin's wonderful lamp."

Faced with the new fortifications, the British had no choice but to evacuate Boston. On March 17, joined by approximately 1,000 Loyalists, the army of General Gage sailed away in almost 170 ships. Colonists who remained loyal to England were called Loyalists or Tories, while those who wanted independence were called Patriots, Rebels, or Whigs.

The Patriots rushed triumphantly into the city and sought revenge against any Loyalists still remaining. They burned some of their homes and stripped, tarred, and feathered the owners, then rode them out of town on rails. The homes of other Loyalists were auctioned off to the highest bidders.

Loyalists were hunted down throughout the colonies, whipped and driven through the streets, or made to get on their knees and denounce the king and his ministers. Washington even wanted to hang some as an example to others.

In the months and years to come, the bitterness would grow between Americans fighting for independence and the almost equal number who remained loyal to England.

The numbers of those who wanted independence were growing, though, thanks in part to a pamphlet called *Common Sense*. Written and published by Thomas Paine in 1776, it was the most successful political pamphlet ever published and sold an estimated 120,000 copies during the first three months.

While leaders and ordinary colonists had ignored Paine's passionate denunciation of African American slavery in his first pamphlet, they heartily approved of his denunciation of royalty and what they feared would be their own enslavement in his second pamphlet.

"The cause of America is in great measure the cause of all mankind," Paine wrote in words that reverberated throughout the colonies. ". . . Freedom hath been hunted around the globe. . . . O receive the fugitive, and prepare in time an asylum for mankind!"

After the publication of *Common Sense*, many colonists understood for the first time just what independence could mean for them.

That understanding did not immediately translate

into enlistments in the Continental Army, however, which still depended for much of its strength on short-term militia units.

Washington moved the army to New York in April, and his men spent the next several weeks fortifying a series of strong points in the city. All able-bodied black men were ordered to help the soldiers, and press gangs rounded up "every Negro that they . . . [met] in the Streets by Day Light. . . ."

Unknown to Washington, a huge force from England was about to rendezvous with General Howe for a massive invasion of New York.

During the weeks Washington was hastily strengthening New York City, Thomas Jefferson was working on the document that would justify the colonists' break with England and King George III: the Declaration of Independence.

Working in a small rented room in Philadelphia while a fourteen-year-old slave he owned named Robert Hemings waited on him, Jefferson wrote: "We hold these truths to be self-evident, that all men are created equal, that they are endowed by their Creator with certain unalienable Rights. . . ."

The words "slave" and "slavery" were so sensitive they did not appear in the document.

To have written openly about American slavery, especially by a man who owned slaves, would have pointed out the contradictions in a document devoted to defending the right of "all" men to be free.

Jefferson had been much more forthright in the Virginia state constitution, which he wrote the month before. In the state constitution, he condemned the king for offering freedom to the slaves by "prompting our negroes to rise in arms against us. . . ."

The delegates must have realized that if all the blame for slavery was placed on the king, they would have no excuse for continuing its practice once the colonies were independent of the king.

Jefferson also accused King George III of trying to turn the "merciless Indian Savages" loose on frontier settlers, even though most conflict with Native Americans occurred when settlers tried to take their land.

The Declaration was approved by Congress on July 4, 1776, with the 56 delegates pledging to each other, "Our Lives, Our Fortunes and our Sacred Honor."

Some colonists attacked the delegates as hypocrites because of the issue of slavery.

"If these solemn *truths*, uttered at such an awful crisis, are *self-evident*," declared Quaker and abolitionist David Cooper, "unless we can shew that the African race are not *men*, words can hardly express the amazement . . . that the very people who make these pompous declarations are slave-holders. . . ."

But that was not the view most colonists held of the Declaration of Independence.

Church bells rang and bonfires blazed throughout the colonies to celebrate its adoption, and the powerful words about equality and unalienable rights quickly took on a life of their own.

This was true for people in all segments of society, including the half of the population Jefferson was not referring to when he wrote about "unalienable Rights": white women, Native Americans, and African Americans.

"I cannot say that I think you very generous to the ladies," Abigail Adams wrote her husband. "For, whilst you are proclaiming peace and good will to men . . . you insist upon retaining an absolute power over wives. But you must remember that arbitrary power is like most other things which are very hard — very liable to be broken. . . ."

African Americans, especially, felt that the words in the Declaration of Independence spoke directly to their deepest hopes and dreams.

African Americans throughout the colonies continued to petition, fight, and run away to gain their own independence. Many in the South made their way to the British, despite Lord Dunmore's defeat, along with white indentured servants who joined them in escaping.

And although there was still an official ban on enlisting slaves in the Continental Army, many ran away and joined by passing themselves off as free men. Still other slaves served in place of their owners.

Slave owners could not only avoid military duty by sending their slaves to the army instead of themselves, but they were also given the slave's enlistment bonus.

The Declaration of Independence was read from Boston's town hall balcony by Thomas Craft, a wealthy merchant who had always opposed violence against the British. Four days later, the Committee of Correspondence ordered townsmen to show up on the Common for a military draft.

When the poorer citizens found that the rich could avoid the draft by paying for substitutes to do their fighting for them, they rioted and shouted: "Tyranny is Tyranny let it come from whom it may!"

In the months and years to come, more and more colonists evaded the draft by sending their slaves to the army instead.

And so it was that an army weakened by deep divisions within colonial society, and overwhelmingly containing the poorer elements of that society, prepared to fight the British.

The British were also deeply divided, however.

The war was so unpopular in England that British leaders hired thousands of Germans to do much of their fighting for them. The Germans came from six principalities, but more than half were from Hesse-Cassel, so the colonists called all of them "Hessians."

Their prince was paid the equivalent of over $500,000 a year for their services, plus $12 for each man wounded and $35 for each man killed.

On June 29, 1776, an American soldier looked out at New York Harbor and saw "something resembling a wood of pine trees. . . . In about ten minutes the whole bay was as full of shipping as ever it could be. . . . I thought all London was afloat."

General William Howe had arrived from Halifax with his invasion fleet, and thirteen days later his brother, Admiral Lord Richard Howe, sailed into the harbor from England.

On August 1, the 3,000-man force of Generals Henry Clinton and Lord Charles Cornwallis also arrived, following an unsuccessful attempt to take Charleston, South Carolina. With them were several black men who had escaped from slavery and were now serving in a Loyalist Virginia militia unit.

The British forces totaled more than 32,000 soldiers, including several regiments of black slaves from the West Indies who had been promised freedom if they fought for England.

The British also had approximately 10,000 sailors, 2,000 Royal Marines, more than 70 warships, and about

400 troops transports. By comparison, Washington had less than 14,000 men healthy and ready to fight, and thousands of these had only a few weeks left to serve.

Realizing that the British would probably try to seize the 100-foot-tall Heights in Brooklyn overlooking Manhattan Island and the harbor, Washington rushed 5,000 troops across the East River to defend them. He also moved his headquarters to the Heights.

Three of the scores — and possibly hundreds — of black soldiers about to fight the British were Primus Hall, Prince Whipple, and Tobias Gilmore.

Hall was a free, twenty-year-old native of Boston who had been released from his apprenticeship to a shoemaker so he could join the army.

Whipple, whose original name is unknown, was born in Africa of wealthy parents who sent him to the colonies to study when he was ten years old. But the captain of the ship kidnapped him and sold him as a slave to General William Whipple of New Hampshire several years before the Revolutionary War began.

Now Prince served as a Continental Army soldier in exchange for the promise of freedom. His duties included acting as bodyguard to General Whipple, who was one of George Washington's aides.

Gilmore was also a native of Africa, a prince whose name was Shilbogee Turry-Werry. He was sold on an auction block in Newport, Rhode Island, to a Captain Gilmore, and regained his freedom after enlisting in the army in 1776. Gilmore would go on to become one of Washington's bodyguards.

On August 22, the British began landing troops on the southwestern tip of Long Island.

Five days later, in what would be remembered as some of the most brutal action of the war, British troops began smashing their way toward the Heights and Washington's headquarters.

CHAPTER
4

There were 10,000 British troops on Long Island in the main force under General Sir William Howe, another 5,000 under Major General James Grant, and 5,000 Hessians with artillery under Major General Leopold von Heister.

Washington received word of their advance at about midnight and ordered 3,000 men out to stop them. The opposing armies met at dawn, with the leading American soldiers opening fire as they took shelter behind a barn and in an orchard.

The two sides battled for hours, until the main body of British troops surrounded the Americans and scattered them. Five hundred men in one Patriot regiment were surprised and overrun before they could fight back. Another large body of Americans was driven into a deep creek where those who could not swim or "procure anything to buoy them up, sunk."

Several Patriot regiments tried to force their way

As it became increasingly difficult to find men willing to fight in a war known for its brutality, 5,000 black men came to the Continental Army and served throughout the war. (Schomburg Center for Research in Black Culture, New York Public Library)

A black soldier, believed to be Prince Whipple, accompanying George Washington while American troops cross the Delaware River. (Library of Congress)

Washington and Lafayette surveying the suffering troops at Valley Forge. (Brown Brothers)

Lafayette recruited James Armistead to work as a spy and risk his life for the cause of American independence. (Valentine Museum, Richmond, Virginia)

Agrippa Hull fought at Saratoga alongside General Tadeusz Kosciuszko. (Stockbridge Library)

This 1779 painting, one of the most significant art finds of the Bicentennial, depicts an unidentified free black sailor, believed to be a member of the twenty-gun privateer General Washington. (Wide World)

Paul Cuffee spoke out against the inequality that black soldiers faced during the Revolutionary War. (Schomburg Center for Research in Black Culture, New York Public Library)

N | Goodrich Command. | MASS. Militia

Umph' Negro

Appears with the rank o *Pivt* on a

Pay Roll*

for the Continental Establishment for Cap' Enoch Noble's Company of   from the County of Barkshire who march to Bennington in the State of Vermont under the Command of Major William Goodrich to Defend the Frontears on October 23, 1780,

(Revolutionary War,)

dated *Berkshire ss. Sheffield*
        Apr. 18 .., 1781

Establishment pr. Month .... *£ 2*

Time of Engagement.... *Oct. 23 .., 1780*

Time of Discharge .... *Nov 4 ..,17 .*

Distance from home when discharged *62 miles*

Days allowed to return } *3*
at 20 miles pr. Day }

Miles Travel out and home *122*

Sum of milage at 1*d* per mile *10.2*

Whole time of service allow- } *16 days*
ing time to return }

Amount of Wages   *£. 1. 13. 4d*

Amount of Wages and Milage *£. 1. 113. 4.1*

of Rations pr. Day   *1*

of Days Drew no Rations

Price of each ration   *8d*

Amount of Rations ...... *5. 4. 9d.*

Amount of wages milage } *£. 1. 16. .1*
and Rations }

Remarks

MUSTER ROLL OF

PR VATE

UMPH NEGRO OF

THE MASSACHUSETTS

M L TIA, 78 .

This payroll statement for "Umph Negro" indicates that he fought for the Massachusetts Militia under the command of Major William Goodrich. (Negro Historical Association)

Some of the Revolutionary War's worst horrors were endured by prisoners on ships such as the Jersey. *(Wide World)*

This illustration of the Jersey's *interior shows a British soldier guarding the prisoners. (Library of Congress)*

Black Revolutionary War soldiers fight against an attack from British troops.

The Battle of Cowpens was a humiliating defeat for Banastre "Butcher" Tarleton, one of the Continental Army's most hated foes. (South Carolina State House, Columbia, South Carolina)

through a woods "where they, almost to a man, were killed," remembered one rifleman.

"It looked horrible in the wood," said a Hessian colonel named von Heeringen, "as at least two thousand killed and wounded lay there."

Groups of Americans were surrounded, then stabbed to death as the circles closed methodically around them.

Many men had broken and run at the first sound of fighting, leading Washington to exclaim: "Good God! Are these the men with whom I am to defend America?"

The battle was over by noon, with the surviving American soldiers retreating into the fortifications at Brooklyn Heights. Half the army was now trapped: In front of them was the British army, and behind them was the water filled with English warships.

Washington considered trying to hold out against the British, but several officers persuaded him the army would be destroyed if he kept it in Brooklyn. And so, on the night of August 29, he began moving the army back to Manhattan in boats rowed by soldiers who were fishermen from Salem and Marblehead, Massachusetts.

They belonged to a regiment commanded by Colonel John Glover. According to one man, Glover's regiment contained "a number of negroes, which, to persons unaccustomed to such associations, had a disagreeable, degrading effect."

There is no record of anyone refusing to ride in the boats because black men helped row them, however.

Many of the boats were so packed with men, they rode just inches above the water. Heavy rain and thick fog helped hide the retreat from the British.

The last boat, with Washington in it, was just pulling away from Brooklyn as daylight came and the British reached the water. The entire American army had escaped the trap, but their losses in the Battle of Brooklyn (often called the Battle of Long Island) had been heavy.

The battle had been the bloodiest the war would see, and involved more total troops than would be seen again on any one battlefield in the war. American losses were over 200 killed and wounded, and almost 900 captured.

Total British casualties were over 900, with most of those being wounded. A large percentage of the wounded on both sides died. This would happen throughout the war because doctors could do little to treat infections that set in with wounds.

The Americans who died after returning to New York were buried in mass graves near the southern tip of Manhattan. Black and white soldiers were buried separately, according to evidence found seventy-five years later.

The Reverend Theodore Parker, a nineteenth century theologian and social reformer, said that when one of the burial spots in Manhattan was excavated so a store could be built, a great quantity of skulls were "thrown up by the workmen."

The skulls, and the bones buried with them, turned out to be the remains "of colored American soldiers, who fell in the disastrous battles of Long Island."

Parker said the bones "of these forgotten victims of the Revolution" were "carted off, and shot into the sea, as the rubbish of the town. Had they been white men's relics, how would they have been honored. . . ."

Washington now realized that his weakened, dispirited, and rapidly dwindling army could not hold New York City against a strong British attack.

Instead of trying to defend the city with his "almost broke down" army as Congress ordered, he proposed burning the town so the British would be unable to use it for winter quarters. But Congress refused to give him permission for such a drastic step.

On September 15, Howe attacked again. There were so many British Redcoats being loaded from warships into troop transports, declared one awed Patriot private, they looked like a "clover field in full bloom."

From dawn till 11 A.M., the British made preparations to attack the middle of Manhattan with 4,000 troops, but nobody bothered to tell Washington about it.

When the warships opened up with what one of their officers called "the most tremendous peal I ever heard," and their troops began coming ashore, the American soldiers panicked and fled.

Washington, hearing the sounds of battle, came riding up "with all possible expedition . . . and, to my great surprize and Mortification, I found the troops . . . running away in the most shameful and disgraceful manner. I used every purpose to rally them but . . . they ran off without firing a Single Gun."

The next day Washington and his officers helped rally the troops as they successfully fought their way to the northern end of Manhattan. There they took shelter behind entrenchments on the Harlem Heights.

Two days later a great fire broke out in New York and destroyed nearly a quarter of the city. Angry British soldiers who suspected Patriots of deliberately setting the fire, threw one man into a burning house and hung another "by the neck till he was dead and afterwards by the heels. . . ."

Washington had sent twenty-four-year-old Captain Nathan Hale to Long Island to spy on British troop movements. Hale was a schoolteacher in civilian life and an officer in the regiment that included Private Jude "Old Rock" Hall and several other black soldiers.

Hale was captured by the British the night of the fire

and confronted by Howe the next day. The furious general took out his anger on Hale, ordering that he be hanged as a spy the next day. He even refused Hale's request to speak to a clergyman or read from a Bible.

A gallows was hastily built, and as Hale stood on it with a noose around his neck, he declared: "I only regret that I have but one life to lose for my country."

His words would become a rallying cry for Patriots in the years to come, but for now they badly needed more than words.

Seeing his army "upon the eve of another dissolution," Washington stressed the urgency of creating a strong "standing Army. Relying so much on short-term militia units," he wrote his brother, Jack, "is, assuredly, resting upon a broken staff."

"Such is my situation," he complained in another letter, "that if I were to wish the bitterest curse to an enemy on this side of the grave, I should put him in my stead with my feelings. . . . In confidence I tell you that I never was in such an unhappy, divided state since I was born."

The weeks that followed brought one American defeat after another, and thousands more soldiers deserted. Against his better judgment, Washington let General Nathanael Greene talk him into leaving almost 3,000 soldiers in Fort Washington, near the highest point in Manhattan.

Three weeks later, Washington and 5,000 of his men

watched helplessly from the New Jersey side of the Hudson as the British captured the fort with almost all its men, 161 cannon, 400,000 cartridges, the soldiers' weapons, and two months' supply of food.

Three days later, the British also captured Fort Lee on the New Jersey side of the Hudson without a fight.

The American army was disappearing before Washington's eyes. Starting with the Battle of Brooklyn, nearly 4,500 of his soldiers had been taken prisoner, thousands more had died of disease or deserted, and hundreds had been killed or wounded.

Equally worrying for him in some ways must have been the fact that many members of Congress and some of his own officers were beginning to doubt his ability to lead.

His trusted friend and aide, General Joseph Reed, complained about Washington to the man who wanted to replace him: General Charles Lee, the second-highest-ranking officer in the army.

Lee promptly thanked Reed for his "flattering letter," and then, referring to Washington, said: "I . . . lament with you that fatal indecision of mind which in war is a much greater disqualification than stupidity, or even want of personal courage."

Washington and the army continued their weary retreat, slowly moving south through New Jersey in raw cold and heavy rains that turned their paths into ribbons of deep, sucking mud. They trudged through the Watchung Mountains, Newark, and New Brunswick, with British pursuers just a day behind.

As the Continental Army retreated through New Jersey, the state's Patriot militia disintegrated and 3,000 citizens took an oath of allegiance to King George.

One of the men who swore allegiance to the king was a black man named Titus, who had escaped from slavery to Lord Dunmore the year before. Now Titus was in New Jersey calling himself Colonel Tye and leading a band of black men and white men that terrorized Patriot farms in northern New Jersey. He would fight his own revolution for five more years, and finally die of battle wounds.

The soldiers still with Washington were among the most steadfast he would ever command, but there were barely 3,000 of them.

One of them was a young man named Peter Jennings, who had been a baker in civilian life. Jennings served in a unique outfit that has left few records behind: Colonel Edward Olney's 5th Regiment (Rhode Island) of Artillery of Blacks.

The war would see two or three black or mostly-black units, but the vast majority of African Americans in the Continental Army served in units that were predominantly white.

Prince Whipple was still one of that ragged band of

Patriots. Oliver Cromwell also continued to shoulder his musket, along with Salem Poor, Primus Hall, Philip Rodman, Cato Prince, and Jude Hall.

On December 8, with the British close on their heels, the army crossed the Delaware River into Pennsylvania in what one soldier described as "the most hellish scene I ever saw." He noticed a soldier walking toward him who "had lost all his clothes . . . and his face so full of sores he could not clean it."

Then the stranger called his name, and he realized he was looking at his brother.

Washington ordered all boats destroyed or brought to the Pennsylvania side of the river for a distance of 60 miles, so the British pursuers could not cross over. He knew the action would not delay them for long, however.

Enlistments were scheduled to expire at the end of the month, and on December 18, 1776 — from his camp "near the Falls of Trenton" — Washington wrote his brother that "if every nerve is not strain'd to recruit the New Army with all possible expedition, I think the game is pretty nearly up. . . ."

And two days later, he warned Congress that "10 days more will put an end to the existence of our Army. . . ."

Searching desperately for a victory that would keep the cause of independence alive and boost the morale of his troops, Washington decided to attack the Hessians at Trenton on the day after Christmas.

Gathering his men on the shores of the Delaware River, he ordered that parts of Thomas Paine's *The American Crisis* be read aloud to them: "These are the times that try men's souls: The summer soldier and the sunshine patriot will, in this crisis, shrink from the service of his country; but he that stands it NOW, deserves the love and thanks of man and woman."

The first of 2,400 American troops began crossing the river from Pennsylvania to New Jersey on Christmas afternoon, leaving a trail in the snow "tinged with the blood from the feet of the men who wore broken shoes," said one of the soldiers.

"It is fearfully cold and raw," wrote Colonel John Fitzgerald, adding: "It will be a terrible night for the soldiers who have no shoes . . . but I have not heard a man complain."

In a scene made famous by the painting *Washington Crossing the Delaware*, the general headed across the river in a rowboat at about 8 P.M. as the wind and ice increased, and the temperature dropped below freezing. Pictured in the boat with him, pulling one of the oars, is a black soldier who is said to be Prince Whipple.

In yet another painting involving the crossing, Washington is shown astride his white horse on the snow-covered banks of the river. Attending him are four other horsemen — three white officers and, again, a black soldier who apparently was Whipple.

It was 3 A.M. before the men managed to get the artillery across, and almost 4 A.M. by the time they started the nine mile march to Trenton in driving sleet that "cut like a knife," said Colonel Fitzgerald.

At broad daylight the Americans encountered their first Hessian troops about a mile outside of Trenton: a handful of sentries who fired and ran.

The fleeing men aroused the garrison in Trenton, but the soldiers — still groggy from their Christmas celebrations the day before — had little time to react. They came running out of houses and tried to form into battle lines while drums beat, a bugle sounded, and cannon roared. American artillery swept the streets with grapeshot, and American riflemen fired from behind fences and houses or charged with fixed bayonets.

The fighting was over in less than an hour, and the result was a stunning Patriot victory. Over 900 Hessians were captured, about two dozen killed, and 84 wounded. American losses were just 4 killed and 8 wounded.

The soldiers also captured forty hogsheads of rum which, as usual, they quickly opened (John Adams would write that "rum was the Spirit of '76").

Washington ordered his weary army back to the

boats for another bitter crossing of the Delaware, with Colonel Glover's regiment once more manning the oars. Three more men froze to death on the journey, but by early evening the others were safely back on the Pennsylvania side.

The British, under Lord Cornwallis, were now pursuing them with 5,500 crack troops and another 2,500 on their way. The Continental Army was down to about 1,600, but Washington suddenly received word that over 3,000 Patriot militiamen had arrived on the New Jersey side of the river.

He was afraid to leave them alone to face the British, but also afraid to risk another river crossing to join them. Battered and bruised though his army was, Washington decided to gamble and take the offensive.

On the night of December 30, he ordered his men to make their third crossing of the Delaware in three days. When they arrived in their new camp, he promised a $10 bounty to anyone who would agree to stay for six more weeks after their enlistment expired.

A drummer boy beat a long roll, waiting for someone to step forth, but at first no one accepted the offer. Then one soldier stepped forward, and was finally followed by about 1,200 others.

The Patriots clashed with the British at twilight near a bridge between Trenton and Princeton. Three times the British tried to fight their way across, but Patriot musket and artillery fire killed or wounded more than a third of them.

"The bridge looked red as blood," said Sergeant Joseph White, "with their killed and wounded, and their red coats."

Cornwallis decided to wait until morning to launch the final attack he felt certain would catch "the old fox," as he called Washington. But during the night the Americans silently pulled out and headed for Princeton.

They left their campfires burning so the British would think they were still there, and muffled the wheels of the cannon so they would make no noise.

The first American detachment to meet the British at Princeton broke and ran after hand-to-hand combat and the killing of their commander. Next the militia, coming on their first scene of battle with its dead and dying men, also turned and ran.

Just then Washington rode up with his Continental Army veterans, and they stood and fought. For several minutes the two sides fired away with muskets and cannon while they stood within 30 yards of each other. But finally the British, fearing they were about to be overwhelmed, fled for their lives.

"It's a fine fox chase, boys!" Washington cried to his men as he galloped after the Redcoats.

Another officer, Colonel Stephen Moylan, said:

"When pursuing the flying enemy it is unnutter-able, inexpressible . . . we trod on air, it was a glorious day."

Oliver Cromwell joined in the chase, declaring later that he and the others "knocked the British about lively."

Primus Hall pursued several British soldiers more than half a mile and captured them single-handed.

The battle lasted less than an hour and by the end of it the Americans had destroyed one of the best units in the British army: the 600-man strong Fourth Brigade. American losses were only 44 dead.

The American soldiers looted the houses in Princeton, as both sides routinely looted in most towns where they fought. They even ate the breakfasts the British soldiers had been about to have when they were attacked.

Washington let the soldiers help themselves to food, clothing, and shoes, then ordered them to burn the rest. He then formed them up again and started toward the main British supply depot at New Brunswick, 19 miles away.

But the worn-out soldiers began dropping out to sleep in barns and silos, and Washington realized he would have too few men to capture the town. He de-cided to head north instead and set up his winter camp in the wooded hills of Morristown, New Jersey. From there he could keep an eye on British movements in

New York and guard the road between Philadelphia and New England.

The decision to turn back from New Brunswick was a bitter blow for him, however.

Just a few hundred "fresh Troops upon a forced March would have destroyed all their Stores, and Magazines," he wrote Congress, "taken . . . their Military Chest containing £70,000 and put an end to the War."

Now the end to the war was years away, but finally it seemed like the Americans had a chance of winning. In September, Congress had adopted the name "The United States of America," and would soon make the Stars and Stripes the new nation's official flag.

By the time the spring of 1777 arrived, the Continental Army had grown to 8,000 strong. Most of the soldiers were still untrained, and a greater number than ever were African Americans.

All of the young Patriots — black and white — would soon have their courage tested in some of the bitterest battles of the war for independence.

CHAPTER

5

In 1777, most African Americans who joined the army were already free. The majority were from New England and were cheaper to enlist than white men because they were paid smaller bonuses.

Although it would soon became almost impossible to persuade appreciable numbers of whites to enlist for a bonus of $1,000 (paid in increasingly worthless Continental money), black soldiers enlisted for bonuses that rarely exceeded $100.

And so African Americans marched off to war from scores of towns and villages throughout the North.

They came from Barrington, Newmarket, Epping, Exeter, Northwood, Stratham, Durham, and Kingstown in New Hampshire. In Connecticut, they joined up from Bridgeport, Colchester, Hartford, Litchfield, and 23 other communities.

Lancaster in Massachusetts sent 14 black men to the war. Medford and Andover also recruited African

Americans, while the Indian district of Marshpee on Cape Cod sent 27 of its residents to the army.

The Marshpee men were mostly of mixed Marshpee and African heritage, and included Francis Websquish, Demps Squibs, Castel Barnet, Hosea Poguit, John Mapix, Mark Negro, and 19 others. They formed a separate company in the army and all but one of them died in the war.

In the South, Virginia enlisted more African Americans than any other state. The number was so high in proportion to the whites sent to fight, Governor Thomas Nelson, Jr., wrote Washington, "as it was thought that they could best be spared."

One of these black Virginians was the appropriately-named Shadrack Battle, who would go on to serve three years in the Continental Army.

So it was that the army that gathered at Morristown, New Jersey, in the second year of the war, was composed mainly of the poor. Many even brought their wives and children with them because the dependents had no other means of support.

By the summer of 1777, the army had grown to about 16,000 soldiers and Washington was worried about its ability to move and fight encumbered by so many civilians (although he added to the number by bringing at least five more slaves from Mount Vernon to take care of his needs).

"In the present marching state of the army," Washington wrote on August 4, "every encumbrance proves greatly prejudicial to the service; the multitude of women in particular, especially those who are pregnant and have children, are a clog upon every movement. . . ."

But throughout the first part of summer, the soldiers at Morristown did little moving as Washington held them in readiness to counter a possible British offensive. To the north, however, American troops were fighting in Rhode Island, Vermont, and upstate New York.

General Lee had been captured by the British several months before and the Americans came up with a plan to capture a British general and exchange him for Lee.

On the night of July 9, 1777, an American commando force of about forty volunteers silently rowed their way toward the British headquarters at Newport, Rhode Island. The headquarters was in a house owned by a Quaker named Overing.

The commandos' oars were muffled so the five boats would not be heard as they passed warships. Leading the raid was Lieutenant Colonel William Barton.

One of the boats was steered by a black man named Tack Sisson as they "passed the enemy's forts," slipped through his "ships of war," and landed near the headquarters of British Major General Richard Prescott.

Sisson — described as "a stout active Negro" —

joined Colonel Barton and one other commando in quickly overpowering the single sentry standing guard.

Then, with "the rest of the men surrounding the house, the Negro, with his head, at the second stroke, forced a passage into it, and then into the general's chamber . . . the colonel calling the general by name, told him he was a prisoner, he replied he knew it. . . ."

Sisson's role in the capture of Prescott was quickly celebrated throughout the colonies in song and verse, all of which ridiculed the general.

One song, which was reportedly composed by a Newport sailor and sung in person to Prescott, ran:

> A tawney son of Afric's race
> Them through the ravine led,
> And entering the Overing house,
> They found him in his bed. . . .
> But to get in they had no means
> Except poor Cuffee's head,
> Who beat the door down, then rushed in,
> And seized him in his bed. . . .

The capture of Prescott, with Sisson using his head to break down the door, brought "great joy and exultation" throughout the colonies, declared one officer.

Congress awarded an elegant sword to Colonel Barton for the capture but, as far as is known, gave nothing to Sisson. The news was also greeted warmly by Washington, who needed all the good news he could get.

"No army was ever worse supplied than ours," he wrote Congress from Morristown.

The average soldier, Washington complained, hadn't tasted a vegetable in over seven months and was paid so little he couldn't afford to buy soap, resulting in a "dirtiness [that] adds not a little to the disease of the Army. . . ."

Even worse, the number of deserters was so great he was trying to figure out "the most effectual means . . . for the recovery of Deserters," including giving rewards to local sheriffs to "apprehend . . . discipline and march them to the Army. . . ."

Unfortunately for Washington and his soldiers, conditions were just as bad when they were again forced into battle.

The Patriots learned that General Howe had sailed from New York City with almost 17,000 soldiers on more than 260 warships and troop transports. Washington feared he was headed for Philadelphia, the seat of the Continental Congress, but was uncertain.

By the last week in August, however, there was no doubt. Howe began landing his troops on the northern shore of the Chesapeake Bay in Maryland, so they could march on Philadelphia. Washington hurried south to block them with an army that had at most 11,000 men fit for duty.

Barzillai Lew from Bunker Hill was still with him, along with Jude "Old Rock" Hall and Sanford Talbert, who had called his all-night work on the fortifications at Breed's Hill "the hottest day's work he had ever done."

But many other veterans had gone home, and their places were now taken by men who had never fought a battle.

Washington prepared to stop the British at a crossing southwest of Philadelphia called Chad's Ford. Pennsylvania officers had assured him that there was no other place for at least a dozen miles where the Brandywine Creek could be waded.

But Howe had surveyed the area in person and knew there was another crossing only seven miles away. At 4 A.M. on September 11, he began marching the main part of his army of 12,000 toward that unsuspected crossing and the rear of the American army.

It was the same strategy he had used with such devastating effect on Long Island, and Washington would again be unprepared for it.

The two sides began to exchange cannon and musket fire in the morning, but it was late afternoon before the main armies collided. The roar of that collision could be heard in Philadelphia more than 20 miles away, and the Continental lines reeled before the onslaught.

Entire regiments of raw recruits fled when they saw thousands of British and Hessian soldiers advancing to the sound of martial music, with bayonets glistening in the morning light.

But in the center of the line, 3,000 American veterans stood and fought. Five times they were beaten from one hill and five times they came charging back. They were joined by a young French nobleman named the Marquis de Lafayette, who tried to rally them although he was already wounded in the leg.

At one point, when the exhausted American army was about to be swept away, two brigades came charging to their rescue. One of the brigades, that of Colonel Peter Muhlenberg, contained almost a hundred African Americans.

These fresh American troops gave their weary comrades time to re-form and to eventually make a skillful, fighting retreat.

Other men were also fighting valiantly.

Thirty-three-year-old Edward Hector, an African-American private in the Third Pennsylvania Artillery, was ordered to abandon his ammunition wagon and join his company's retreat.

"The enemy shall not have my team," he replied. "I will save my horses, or perish myself!"

Hector proceeded to gather up the guns his retreating comrades had abandoned, then calmly left the field with their weapons and the ammunition wagon.

Another black soldier, John Francis of the Third Pennsylvania Regiment, was shot in both legs and "much shattered by grape shot."

Some British soldiers had brutally murdered a schoolteacher near Chad's Ford the day before the battle. Now one of the Americans fighting on the battlefield was a huge black man who had been befriended by the schoolteacher and his daughter. The schoolteacher had taught him when he asked to learn and the daughter had fed him when he was hungry.

Known only to history as Black Samson, he slashed his way through the British Redcoats wielding a scythe, determined to avenge the teacher's death.

Black Samson, said one man, "swept his way through the red ranks like a sable figure of Time."

Over a hundred years later, poet Paul Laurence Dunbar would write:

> Straight through the human harvest,
>   Cutting a bloody swath,
> Woe to you, soldier of Briton!
>   Death is abroad in his path.
> Flee from the scythe of the reaper,
>   Flee while the moment is thine,

None may with safety withstand him,
Black Samson of Brandywine.

Night finally came for the battered American troops. Washington knew his soldiers could not win, so he ordered a withdrawal under cover of darkness, just as the army had withdrawn under cover of darkness after the Battle of Brooklyn.

The American losses were estimated at 200 killed, 400 wounded, and 500 captured. The British lost only 90 killed, 448 wounded, and 6 missing.

With the road to Philadelphia now wide open, Howe marched triumphantly into the city a few days later as its Loyalist residents cheered. Washington, on the other hand, was the object of intense criticism.

"O, Heaven! grant us one great soul!" John Adams cried, even as he and other congressmen fled in panic from Philadelphia to York, Pennsylvania.

"Before I came to the army," declared the new adjutant general, Timothy Pickering, to General Nathanael Greene, "I entertained an exalted opinion of General Washington's military talents, but I have since seen nothing to enhance it."

Determined to stop the rising storm of criticism and seeing an opportunity to catch the British by surprise, Washington ordered an attack at Germantown a few miles north of Philadelphia.

Just after a misty sunrise on October 4, Washington's force of 11,000 Continental Army soldiers and militiamen attacked the British garrison of 12,000.

The force was divided into four columns, and at first all went well, even though Adam Stephen, one of the generals commanding the militia, was drunk.

But then a heavy fog rolled in and the soldiers began to panic.

The confused Americans shot at trees, fences, and the dark silhouettes of their own men, and many soon ran out of ammunition.

If the fog had not come, Washington wrote his brother, "we should, I believe, have made a decisive and glorious day of it . . . [but] it was a bloody day. Would to Heaven I could add, that it had been a more fortunate one for us."

Washington estimated that about a thousand Americans were killed, wounded, captured, or missing, "but of the missing, many, I dare say, took advantage of the times, and deserted." British losses were about half as much.

The American captives from Germantown joined hundreds of others in a Philadelphia jail, where a fever "Swept off in the course of three months 400 men," wrote one of the prisoners, Lieutenant James Morris of Connecticut, "who were all buried in one continued Grave without Coffins . . . three deep one upon another. . . . Death was so frequent that it ceased to terrify. It ceased to warn; it ceased to alarm. . . ."

Caesar Clark, Peter Jennings, Jack Rowland, and Shadrack Battle were some of the African-American soldiers who came through the Battle of Germantown unscathed.

Another was Caesar Shelton, who had been born at sea while his mother — a free woman — was journeying to an unknown destination. The captain betrayed her and sold both her and her newborn son into slavery for life. Now Shelton was fighting as a substitute for his slave owner in return for a promise of freedom.

Not all black soldiers at Germantown were as fortunate as Shelton and the others, however. One of the Patriot dead was a black youth from New York named Benjamin Whitecuff.

Whitecuff was a free man whose father served as a sergeant in the Continental Army and who had persuaded his son to enlist, after another son became a spy for the British.

In peacetime the three had worked side by side on the father's farm. Now the Patriot son lay in a grave on the Germantown battlefield.

The gloom of yet another defeat hung heavy over the American army, but Washington and his men also knew they had come within a hair's breadth "of grasping a compleat victory," as the commander in chief put it, over some of the best soldiers in the world.

Then news came from the North that brought joy to the heart of every Patriot from Washington to the lowliest soldier in the ranks. A British army of over 6,000 under the command of General John Burgoyne had surrendered at Saratoga in upstate New York.

Suddenly the Patriot dream of independence seemed more real than ever before. It was as if the blood that had been shed at Lexington and Concord, Bunker Hill, Brooklyn, Trenton, Princeton, Brandywine, and Germantown was at last giving rise to a new nation.

Benedict Arnold was the hero at Saratoga, leading one fearless charge after another until he was finally stopped by a musket ball through the leg.

Peter Salem was at Saratoga, wielding the same gun he had used so effectively at Bunker Hill. John Peterson, who would later help foil a plot by Benedict Arnold to turn over West Point to the British, was there.

And among the many other African Americans who fought at Saratoga were Agrippa Hull, who could usually be found at the side of Polish volunteer, General Tadeusz Kosciuszko; Wentworth Cheswell, a volunteer who had marched all the way from New Hampshire with his white comrades; Luke Nickelson, one of the dozens of Americans wounded at Saratoga; and Cuff

Whitemore, the veteran who had been among the last to leave the redoubt at Bunker Hill.

"You never see a regiment in which there are not a lot of negroes, and there are well-built, strong, husky fellows among them," wrote a captured Hessian officer.

The Battle of Saratoga was one of the decisive moments in history. As a result of the victory, France declared war on England and promised the full support of its powerful army and navy to the American cause. A year later, Spain and Holland did the same.

Congress proclaimed December 18 as a day of Thanksgiving for the victory at Saratoga, but the only food available for most soldiers to celebrate with was four ounces of rice and a tablespoon of vinegar provided, said one sarcastic soldier, by "Our country, [which] ever mindful of its suffering army, opened her sympathizing heart so wide. . . ."

The next day, December 19, 1777, Washington led about 11,000 men to their winter encampment on a thickly wooded slope two miles long overlooking the Schuylkill River in Pennsylvania. The site was about 20 miles from Philadelphia and was destined to go down in American history as the embodiment of courage, suffering, and endurance: Valley Forge.

More than 2,000 of the men had no shoes, and the frozen trail to Valley Forge was red with the blood from their feet. The last of the soldiers reached the site at nightfall and the next day began building the 1,000 huts where they would spend the winter crowded a dozen or more into a space the size of an average room.

Some of the men were accompanied by their wives, sisters, or mothers, who either lived with them or boarded with local families.

There was little food and clothing, and many men wondered why they should continue to fight for a nation and a Congress that cared so little about them.

Just four days after the army arrived at Valley Forge, Washington wrote Continental Congress President Henry Laurens about a "dangerous mutiny . . . which with difficulty was suppressed by the spirited exertions of our officers. . . ."

Washington said that many men had to sit up all night by the fire because they had no blankets, and that 2,898 men "are now unfit for duty, because they are barefoot and otherwise naked. . . ."

Unless some action was taken quickly to provide the soldiers with food and clothing, he warned, "I am now convinced beyond a doubt, that . . . this army must inevitably be reduced to one or other of these three things; starve, dissolve, or disperse in order to obtain subsistence in the best manner they can."

Three thousand soldiers deserted in the first three months of 1778. Another 1,000 were so ill they could not even leave their huts.

General Anthony Wayne complained bitterly that "the whole army is sick and crawling with vermin."

The twenty-year-old Lafayette said the soldiers "had neither coats nor hats, nor shirts or shoes; their feet and legs froze until they grew black and it was often necessary to amputate them."

Men doing guard duty often stood on their hats to keep their bare feet out of the snow. Worst of all for the soldiers, however, was their constant hunger.

Farmers refused to sell to the army in exchange for Continental currency. Instead, almost every day they drove wagon loads of provisions past Valley Forge to sell to the British for gold.

A free black farmer named Benjamin Banneker, who would later publish his own almanacs and help survey the nation's capital in the District of Columbia, smuggled food through British lines to the soldiers at Valley Forge.

Washington promised to share in his soldiers' hardships "and partake of every inconvenience."

In reality, however, he moved into a snug stone house in early January. The next month his wife, Martha, came up from Mount Vernon. Slaves and servants tended to the couple's needs.

But Washington seemed genuinely concerned about "the naked and distressed Soldier," and watched anxiously as the army once more melted away. More than 1,000 of his soldiers deserted to the British during the winter of 1778, and another 3,000 died of starvation, exposure, typhus, pneumonia, smallpox, dysentery, and other illnesses.

Every morning "meat wagons" creaked slowly through the camp, collecting the bodies of men who had died during the night. Members of burial details often fought the dead soldier's comrades for his shoes because even if the shoes could not be worn, they could be boiled and eaten.

Farmers in New York sold their grain to New England and to the British army in New York City because of higher profits, and Boston merchants refused to sell uniforms to the army for less than 1,000 to 1,800 percent profit.

General Anthony Wayne tried to buy uniforms for his soldiers out of his own pocket, but the clothier general refused to authorize the purchase because it was "irregular."

As a last resort to feed and clothe his men, Washington sent armed foraging parties into the countryside, seizing what food could be found and raiding local mills for cloth.

What little food and clothing actually reached Valley Forge from government suppliers was often useless because of the corruption of those supplying it. Coats arrived without buttons and food was so poor it became the butt of grim jokes among the half-starved men.

Washington sought desperately to find new soldiers while trying to hold on to the ones he had.

The states were not only failing to meet their Continental Army quotas, but those in the South were still more determined to protect slavery than fight for independence (Massachusetts would end up sending more troops to the army during the war than all the Southern states combined).

In Virginia, Patrick Henry used much of his military manpower to stop slaves and indentured servants from running away. The Georgia assembly required that one third of its troops remain in the state as a permanent slave patrol.

But Washington, with the cries of his cold and

suffering soldiers all around him and his army disappearing, still hesitated to strengthen the Continental ranks by enlisting slaves in exchange for their freedom.

Desperation was leading him to consider employing African Americans to transport supplies to the army, however.

"The difficulty of getting waggoners and the enormous wages given them would tempt one to try any expedient to answer the end on easier and cheaper terms," he wrote Congress. "Among others it has occurred to me, whether it would not be eligible to hire negroes in Carolina, Virginia and Maryland for the purpose. They ought however to be freemen for slaves . . . would too frequently desert to the enemy to obtain their liberty. . . ."

The slave trade was the source of most of Rhode Island's wealth. Toward the end of 1776 the British had captured Newport, the state's great slave port and, next to Boston, New England's busiest port. Thousands of citizens fled the state as British troops plundered their wealth.

By the early part of 1778, one fourth of the best farmland was controlled by the British, the state's 400 miles of undefended coastline had been ravaged, 6,000 British soldiers occupied Newport, and much of the population was on the verge of starvation.

Three Continental Army brigades were sent to protect the state, but their enlistments were about to expire.

General James Mitchell Varnum of Rhode Island told Washington that a battalion of whites could not be raised in the state. Instead, he suggested enlisting slaves, assuring Washington that "a battalion of Negroes can easily be raised. . . ."

Rhode Island legislators approved of the plan, telling Washington it would be impossible to fill the state's quota "without arming the slaves."

Varnum, who was also a delegate to the Continental Congress, suggested that three Rhode Island officers at Valley Forge be sent home at once to recruit the black soldiers. In exchange for joining, slaves were to be given their freedom and all the Continental bounties and wages given white soldiers.

To overcome the objections of slave owners, the state promised to pay them the full value of any slave who joined the army.

The proposal may well have startled Washington, whose official writings largely avoided the subject of arming slaves, but he allowed the experiment to go forward.

But unlike Washington, several other American officers were eager to link the struggle for independence with the opportunity to end slavery.

One of these officers was Major John Laurens of

South Carolina, son of the politically powerful Henry Laurens. Serving as a volunteer aide to Washington at Valley Forge, the younger Laurens wrote his father about a plan to enlist Southern slaves, which he called "an untried source."

By arming the slaves in exchange for their freedom, the idealistic young officer declared, "I would bring about a two-fold good: . . . advance those who are unjustly deprived of the rights of mankind . . . and . . . have a corps of such men . . . ready in every respect to act at the opening of the next campaign."

Washington did not give his approval for the plan, but the Rhode Island plan had his full support.

Colonel Christopher Greene hurried north from Valley Forge to help create one of the most extraordinary units in the Revolutionary War: the "Black Regiment of Rhode Island."

The first three recruits were sworn in near the end of February, and in the months that followed more than 200 others arrived from almost 20 towns and villages throughout the state. Some of the recruits were already free, but the majority were slaves who were declared "absolutely free" as soon as they joined up.

The regiment was authorized to enlist "every able-bodied Negro, Mulatto or Indian Man slave" in the state, but apparently most of the men who joined were described as "Negro."

Dick Champlin, Edward Rose, and Isaac Rodman came from South Kingstown to join, while Query Sweeting made his way to the regiment from Providence, Rutter Gardner from Exeter, Jacob Hazard from Jamestown, and John Burroughs from Newport.

Officially designated the First Rhode Island Regiment, it would see five consecutive years of service, a record equaled by few other regiments in the war. Soon Colonel Greene and the men in the "Black Regiment" would prove they were as brave as any soldiers in the Continental Army, and braver than many.

During the early months of 1778, however, as the raw recruits arrived to begin what one officer would call their "long service and sufferings," the Patriot cause seemed almost hopeless.

At Valley Forge, the groans of the sick and hungry continued to ring from the huts, along with the cry: "No bread, no soldier! No bread, no soldier!"

When the enlistments of 1,000 Virginia soldiers expired, only forty signed up for another term, despite Patrick Henry's offer of an extra bonus to any who reenlisted.

Gradually, a few new men arrived, including some described by a Pennsylvania farmer, who wrote in his diary: "From New England there arrived a company of soldiers, composed of whites, blacks and a few Stockbridge Indians. . . ."

The army slowly grew again, and then, into the gloom that still overhung the encampment, came a man who would transform the Continental Army. He called himself Baron Friedrich Wilhelm von Steuben.

Dressed in a brand-new American uniform with decorations covering his chest, he arrived at Valley Forge in a horse-drawn sleigh with a greyhound dog at his side. Riding on horseback and in a carriage were five grooms and drivers, three servants, three French aides, and one cook.

Actually von Steuben was neither the baron he claimed to be, nor the general, knight, or aide to Frederick the Great he also claimed to be. In reality, he was a former German army captain who had been discharged fifteen years before. He would soon prove, however, that he could do one thing better than anyone else in the American army: turn raw recruits into battle-ready soldiers.

"The men were literally naked," the stunned von Steuben said of the troops who greeted his eyes. "The officers who had coats had them of every color . . . made of an old blanket or a woolen bedcover. With regard to their military discipline, I may safely say no such thing existed."

But soon it would.

Baron von Steuben, who could speak little English, began drilling the men in the basics of marching and handling weapons.

Shouting out such orders as "Doo der rear, march!" and chanting a cadence of "Vun-doo-dree-four," he soon had the men laughing at him and repeating his accent. At first von Steuben was surprised at their laughter and what he thought was mockery, but the soldiers liked him and the parade ground quickly became a place of fun for soldiers and von Steuben alike.

When the quick-tempered general grew angry and couldn't find the English swear words he wanted, he ordered one of his officers to swear for him, declaring: "I gan gurse dem no more!"

He also used his friendships with other officers as another training tool, casually telling them the soldiers would be more effective if treated with kindness rather than the beatings and whippings routinely used on the powerless in colonial America.

The Continental Army grew steadily more powerful as spring wore on and recruits poured into Valley Forge. The English government made peace overtures, but Washington scorned them.

Sir Henry Clinton had replaced Lord Howe as the British commander in Philadelphia, and in June 1778, he ordered the British soldiers to begin retreating from Philadelphia to New York City (estimates of the number involved range from 10,000 to 15,000).

Clinton had heard that the French fleet was on its way to Philadelphia and feared he could not hold the city in the face of a combined French and American attack.

Washington saw an opportunity to head off the British columns and inflict heavy damage on them. Leaving Benedict Arnold as the military governor of Philadelphia, he left Valley Forge surrounded by a guard of fifty soldiers with drawn swords.

John Laurens was there as was twenty-two-year-old Alexander Hamilton, another aide to Washington who believed that black men should be allowed to fight both for their freedom and the freedom of the colonies. (Hamilton, whose mother was from the West Indies, was rumored to be part-black.)

Approximately 12,000 men marched out behind Washington from the valley they had entered in despair six months before. Both the army and the cause they were ready to die for had been transformed, partly because of von Steuben's training and partly because of the soldiers' own belief in the cause of freedom.

Barzillai Lew, Salem Poor, and Oliver Cromwell were among the soldiers who marched triumphantly out of Valley Forge. Jack Rowland and eleven other African Americans in his Connecticut Regiment were also among the veterans who survived that terrible winter.

But one of the black men who did not march out with his comrades was Private Phillip Field of the Second New York Regiment.

Field was one of the approximately 2,500 American soldiers who died at Valley Forge, succumbing to conditions that filled Lafayette with awe.

No European army, he told a friend during the winter, "would suffer the tenth part of what the Americans suffer."

On June 28 in the village of Monmouth Court House, New Jersey, the American advance division of about 5,400 men caught up with part of the British army. The Americans were commanded by General Charles Lee and the British by Lord Cornwallis.

Lee, who had been released by the British in a prisoner of war exchange a few weeks earlier, was suspected of being a traitor by some American officers and was openly scornful of Washington's military abilities ("not fit to command a sergeant's guard," he declared).

The exhausted British had stopped to rest after a long march in heat that would soon exceed 100 degrees. Despite instructions by Washington to attack, however, Lee seemed confused and ordered some of his troops to retreat.

Lafayette urged an immediate attack, but Lee replied: "Sir, you do not know British soldiers. We cannot stand against them. . . ."

There then followed what Laurens called "a senseless retreat without firing a musket over ground which might have been disputed inch by inch."

A startled Washington galloped toward the village

and met a mass of soldiers who were "flying from a shadow," according to one officer.

Finally spotting General Lee, Washington demanded: "What, Sir, is the meaning of this? Whence come this disorder and confusion?"

Lee had no adequate answer and the infuriated Washington, according to General Charles Scott, "swore . . . till the leaves shook on the trees. . . ."

Whatever Washington's reply, he charged forward, stopped two retreating regiments, and ordered them to turn and fight.

The American soldiers quickly obeyed, holding off "the assault of the whole British line" until Washington could reorganize the main army on "advantageous ground."

Now the Continental Army troops cut loose with their artillery, "The severest cannonading . . . as ever was in America," declared New Hampshire's Colonel Joseph Cilley. "The cannonading lasted between two and three hours. . . ."

The British cannon were firing back.

"The first shot they gave us . . . cut off the thigh bone of a captain, just above the knee," remembered Private Joseph Plumb Martin, "and the whole heel of a private in the rear of him. . . ."

Men were also dropping from heat exhaustion. Private Thomas Camel, who chose to join the army rather than remain a slave, was one of countless soldiers who became "quite fatigued and very sick" during the battle.

Colonel Cilley said temperatures were so high "several of my men died with the heat."

A woman named Mary Ludwig Hayes had accompanied her husband to the battlefield with his artillery unit, gaining the nickname from his comrades of "Molly Pitcher," because she carried pitchers of water to them in the heat.

It was said she smoked, chewed tobacco, and swore "like any trooper."

During the battle her husband was killed and "Molly Pitcher" began firing the cannon in his place.

A few yards away, Samuel Charlton — a native of New Jersey who was serving in the army as a substitute for his slave owner — also fired a cannon at the attacking British. After the battle, Washington was said to have praised both Charlton and "Molly Pitcher," who quickly became the new nation's first heroine.

The American soldiers beat back one assault after another as the day wore on, until the fierce heat and unceasing cannon fire forced the weary British to stop.

Washington ordered a counterattack, but his soldiers were too exhausted to comply. By the time fresh troops arrived, it was dark. The commander in chief made plans to attack at dawn, then slept on his cloak under a large oak tree with Lafayette beside him.

But in the morning, Washington discovered the British had slipped away under cover of darkness, just as he and the American army had slipped away at night from Long Island.

The Americans buried 251 British and Hessian troops, and suffered 69 deaths of their own in the battle. Another 37 Americans died of sunstroke.

The British now also faced extremely high desertion rates.

"Desertions still continue from the enemy at the least confusion," wrote Colonel Cilley after the battle. "Their army is weakened two thousand five hundred since they left Philadelphia. I think Clinton is brought himself into a fine hobble."

Shadrack Battle, Artillo Freeman, Pomp Peters, Sylvester Beverly, and almost all the other black soldiers who fought at the Battle of Monmouth Courthouse came through unscathed, but Thomas Lively — who would serve three more years in the Continental Army, be wounded twice, and eventually be captured — lost his right eye in the fighting.

The Battle of Monmouth Courthouse was another turning point in the Revolutionary War. It was the war's longest battle and the last major engagement in the North. Though both sides could claim victory, the British retreat led to a loss of prestige for them and an increase in confidence for the Patriots.

An official return compiled a few weeks after the battle listed 755 black soldiers in 14 Continental Army brigades, but black soldiers also served in four other brigades that were not included in the report.

The 2nd Pennsylvania Brigade, commanded by General Samuel Parsons, contained the most African Americans, numbering 148 in its ranks.

Two Virginia brigades followed, with 98 black soldiers in one and 89 in the other. The Nickens family — a free, well-to-do African American family in Lancaster County, Virginia — sent at least nine brothers and cousins to the Continental Army, while the free Cumbo family sent four of its men off to fight.

At least seventy-two towns in Massachusetts sent black soldiers to the army, and one Connecticut company was called the "Attucks Company" because all of its members were black.

By 1778, the third year of the war, at least one out of every twenty men in the Continental Army was an African American.

Two months after the Battle of Monmouth Courthouse, they again made their presence felt in what started out as a combined American army and French navy effort to capture Newport, Rhode Island. American and French commanders had major disagreements, however, and the French fleet under Admiral Jean-Baptiste d'Estaing sailed away.

A British force of several thousand then assaulted the withdrawing Americans. The Black Regiment of

Rhode Island formed only a small part of the American force, but a body of Hessians concentrated their fierce assaults on them for almost four hours. Apparently the Germans thought the regiment's members were raw soldiers who would break and run.

"*Three times in succession* were they [the Black Regiment] attacked, with most desperate valor and fury, by well disciplined and veteran troops," declared a white soldier who fought near them, "and *three times* did they successfully repel the assault, and thus preserve our army from capture. . . . They were brave, hardy troops. . . ."

The next day the Hessian commander asked for permission to leave his unit "because he dared not lead his regiment again to battle, lest his men shoot him for having caused so much loss."

Lafayette called the Battle of Rhode Island "the best fought action of the war," even though it ended in an American defeat.

Colonel Greene and the members of the Black Regiment had written their names into history, and in the years to come they would add many more pages.

Black manpower was now becoming more important than ever to both sides. Before 1778 was over, the British would shift their military focus to the South and its two large sources of potential allies: white Loyalists and black slaves.

CHAPTER
7

There was a vast population of slaves in Georgia, South Carolina, and Virginia, and leaders on both sides now tried to figure out how best to use that manpower to gain victory for themselves.

Lord Cornwallis and Sir Henry Clinton once again offered freedom to any slave who would fight for them, and thousands ran away — many to the British and others to any haven they could find.

In a vain attempt to recapture fugitives who had taken refuge on ships anchored in Virginia waters, Patrick Henry sent a delegation of slave owners to the British. Sir George Collier, the English commander, told the slave owners that while his men were not trying to persuade slaves to run away, they would offer asylum to anyone who sought it.

Slaves had been escaping for over 150 years before the Revolution, but now the number of fugitives was so great it threatened the ability of the Southern colonies to wage war.

Alexander Hamilton, urging that slaves be given their freedom in exchange for becoming soldiers, warned Congress "that if we do not make use of them in this way, the enemy probably will. . . ."

Unless leaders in the South took immediate steps to aid the Continental Army and the cause of independence, Washington declared, "our affairs are irretrievably lost."

Where, he asked angrily, were Jefferson and other Virginia leaders when the Patriot cause was in such desperate need of help?

In December 1778, when the British attacked Savannah, Georgia, the Patriot force under Major General Robert Howe — the only part of the American army in the South — numbered only 700 Continental Army soldiers and 300 militia.

The British were preparing a frontal assault on the American positions when a black man named Quamino Dolly offered to show them a secret way through a swamp. In all likelihood the path had long been used by slaves trying to find freedom for themselves and their families.

The action of Dolly in aiding the British was precisely what Laurens, Hamilton, and others had warned would happen if slaves were not allowed to fight for freedom.

Now a black man who knew the secret path that had led to freedom for fugitive slaves, used it to lead the British to the rear of the unsuspecting Americans.

On December 29, the British under Lieutenant Colonel Archibald Campbell were able to attack from the sides as well as the front, hurling eight battalions at the stunned Patriots.

Four of the battalions were composed of Americans who were siding with the British, including several black men and one battalion of Irish deserters from the Continental Army who called themselves the Volunteers of Ireland.

The British shattered the American force, killing and wounding almost 100 and capturing more than 450.

A jubilant Campbell also reported that his forces captured "the fort, with all its stores . . . and in short, the capital of Georgia. . . ."

British losses were just 7 men killed and 19 wounded.

"I may venture to say," Campbell declared, "that I have ripped one star and one stripe from the Rebel flag of America."

The British now had the base they wanted for attacks throughout Georgia and South Carolina, in what was rapidly becoming a civil war of American against American — especially in the South.

Savannah had barely fallen when 1,400 Georgians rushed to take an oath of allegiance to the king and formed 20 Loyalist companies to fight for the British.

When Campbell pushed his forces into the countryside, so many local inhabitants volunteered to join him he was able to organize them into militia units and scouting parties.

Families, friends, and neighbors were ripped apart as they split on whether or not Americans should be fighting for independence. State legislatures passed harsh laws aimed at British sympathizers: confiscating property, limiting freedom of speech, and deeming it an act of treason punishable by hanging to publicly question the cause of independence.

Congress urged citizens to inform on one another and to terrify those suspected of being disloyal into silence and inaction.

An American militia unit that captured a company of Loyalist volunteers, brought seventy of them before a court on charges of treason and hanged five.

Lord Cornwallis urged the Georgians who rallied behind him to burn the property of "all who refuse to take the oath of allegiance to England," and his Loyalist followers eagerly obeyed.

On a cold winter day in February 1779, a Patriot force under Colonel Elijah Clark clashed with Loyalists in northeast Georgia in an attempt to stop their reign of terror. With the Patriots was a teenaged artilleryman named Austin Dabney, the free son of a white mother and black father.

Dabney was the only black Patriot in the Battle of Kettle Creek, which one man said was "the hardest ever fought in Georgia," and his heroism on that day became legendary.

Over half a century later, a Georgia governor wrote of Dabney: "No soldier under Clark was braver, or did better service during the Revolutionary struggle."

The young man fought until a shot tore through his thigh, crippling him for life, but he helped the Patriots gain a decisive victory. A white soldier named Giles Harris then rescued Dabney and helped nurse him back to health.

The shortage of American troops in the South was so desperate that in March 1779, a congressional committee took the unprecedented step of recommending slave enlistments in South Carolina and Georgia.

Congress recommended that a 3,000-member battalion of slaves be formed, with the men to be given their freedom at the end of the war if they served "well and faithfully." Slave owners would be paid up to $1,000 for "each active able-bodied negro man of standard size, not exceeding thirty-five years of age," that they contributed to the battalion.

To try and overcome fears that arming slaves would lead to a rebellion, some delegates argued that it would actually "lessen the dangers from revolts and desertions, by detaching the most vigorous and enterprising among the negroes."

Congress commissioned Laurens and appointed him lieutenant colonel to head the unit.

"Had we arms for three thousand such black men as I could select in Carolina," he wrote his father, "I should have no doubt of success in driving the British out of Carolina, and subduing East Florida, before the end of July."

But despite his tireless efforts, his plan was "blown up" by South Carolina legislators "with contemptuous huzzas," his father told a friend.

Some legislators were so outraged by the proposal they sent a flag of truce to British General Augustine Prevost, offering to take South Carolina out of the war. Prevost refused to negotiate with them, however, and the South Carolina Patriots were reluctantly forced to continue the fight for independence.

Thousands of slaves were now running away, especially in South Carolina and Georgia. Those captured by the Continental Army were often returned to their owners or sold and the money given to the soldiers.

When a slave named Charles escaped from a Long Island, New York, slave owner with his wife and little daughter, a Continental Army sergeant under the command of Pennsylvania's General Edward Hand returned them to slavery.

Charles then wrote to General Hand that he was "ever ready under your honors command to fight against all Enemys of the Honble. United States in defense of Liberty and the Rights of Mankind."

Charles asked for only one thing: freedom for himself and his family. The fate of Charles and his family is unknown.

By 1779, especially in Southern coastal areas, capturing slaves was an important objective for both sides. Labor was desperately needed for a variety of tasks, from building fortifications to foraging for food, so each side turned to slaves to supply its needs.

Virginia, with Thomas Jefferson as governor, bought black men, women, and children to labor for the state. Some were sent to the lead mines, while others were forced to work as wagoners, armorers, blacksmiths, carpenters, or in the state-owned ironworks where they were put to work molding and casting cannon.

In the spring of 1779, the British carried off 500 black people in Norfolk County, Virginia, and an English officer returning to General Prevost's headquarters in Georgia brought 300 black men, women, and children with him.

When British General Edward Mathew left Virginia in the summer of 1779 to rejoin Clinton in New York City, he carried with him over 500 men, women, and children. All of these slaves were taken from plantations near the waterfront.

Partly because of the need to stop British slave raids, the Patriot navy assumed an increasingly important role in the war.

The navy was divided into three parts and each part welcomed black seamen: the Continental Navy, the state navies, and privateers — privately owned ships commissioned by individual states to act as vessels of war against the British.

Blacks as well as whites preferred to serve on privateers, which were owned by rich merchants. Privateers captured British ships and sold the cargo, dividing the prize money between owners and crew.

John Hancock and Robert Morris, both signers of the Declaration of Independence, made fortunes during the war from the privateers they owned. There were hundreds of privateers, compared with only about 50 Continental Navy ships and a few ships apiece in the navies of each coastal state.

Hundreds of black men served in the U.S. navies during the war, including some who fought as marines. In the North, most of them were freemen from the coast who had long been welcomed aboard the fishing fleets of New England, while in the South many were slaves.

Two of the most famous black seamen during the war were pilots Caesar Tarrant and "Captain" Mark Starlins. Both men were slaves.

Tarrant piloted the armed vessel *Patriot*, when she captured the *Fanny* on its way to Boston with supplies for the British army. He also steered the *Patriot* in a fight south of the Virginia capes, where officers said he "behaved gallantly."

Starlins was a native of Africa who "was brought up as a pilot, and proved a skillful one, and a devoted patriot. . . ."

Because of his bravery during the war, he was said to be highly thought of "by all worthy citizens, and, more particularly, by all the navy officers of the State."

While Tarrant and Starlins patrolled the coasts, rivers, and inlets of the South, another African American was about to write his name into history in the North.

His name was Pompey Lamb and he was a spy, one of several black spies in the American Revolution.

On June 1, 1779, British forces under Clinton captured the American fort at Stony Point, New York, on the banks of the Hudson River north of New York City. The fort was surrounded on three sides by water, with a swamp in the rear. The sides facing the water had steep cliffs that rose 150 feet above the river.

The only way to reach the fort during high tide was by a causeway across the marshy area, and Clinton further reinforced the fort so it was virtually impregnable. He also anchored the sloop of war HMS *Vulture* just offshore to provide additional firepower.

When "Mad" Anthony Wayne proposed to capture Stony Point, his fellow officers thought he was truly crazy. Washington approved of the plan, however, and Wayne prepared to attack using the Continental Army's new elite force: the American Light Infantry. The brigade was a handpicked, well-trained unit of 1,300 men.

Salem Poor was one of these veteran soldiers. Some of the other black men in the American Light Infantry were Thomas Buckner, who would be captured shortly after the attack and imprisoned for several months; George Dias, a Maryland shoemaker in civilian life; and "Father Stanup," soon to be left on the field for dead, only to recover and live a long life in Ohio.

Wayne was still planning his attack when he is said to have learned about Pompey Lamb, who lived on a nearby farm. The legend of what happened next was related by several nineteenth century American writers, including essayist, historian, and short story writer Washington Irving.

Lamb often sold his fresh vegetables and berries to the British soldiers, and was routinely allowed into the fort.

Wayne asked him to start going to the fort at night so the British would give him the secret passwords necessary to enter the fort after dark.

Lamb agreed and told the British he could come only

at night because he had to hoe corn during the day. Not wanting to lose the fresh food, they agreed to this and gave him the secret words: "The fort is our own."

On the night of July 15, 1779, Wayne's men slit the throats of every dog in the area to prevent them from barking and arousing suspicion. Lamb then made his way across the causeway to the first British sentinel, carrying his fruit and vegetables, and accompanied by two American soldiers disguised as farmers.

The black man called out "The fort is our own," and began talking to the relaxed sentinel, even handing him some fruit. Suddenly the soldiers seized the sentinel and gagged him. Then Lamb walked up to a second sentinel stationed nearer the fort. He, too, was quickly seized and gagged, leaving the causeway unprotected.

Wayne and his men were not far behind. Their approach was so silent they were within pistol range of the rest of the guards before the British discovered them.

The shots that followed began a fierce battle that was over in thirty minutes. American soldiers kept yelling "The fort is our own," and in the confusion and panic that followed, British soldiers surrendered wholesale.

The Patriots quickly turned the fort's guns on the *Vulture*, which hoisted anchor and moved rapidly downstream.

All but a handful of the 600 British soldiers in the fort were killed, wounded, or captured, while American losses were just 15 killed and 85 wounded.

Among the British captives were three black men. Instead of selling them as so many American commanders did, however, General Wayne and his officers gave them their freedom.

In the weeks following the capture of Stony Point, American forces conducted an expedition against the Iroquois Confederacy in New York. (The Confederacy, or "Six Nations," was composed of the Mohawk, Oneida, Onondaga, Cayuga, Seneca, and Tuscarora nations.)

The expedition was one of the most brutal military campaigns in American history, and its target was men, women, and children.

Native Americans had been fighting their own "War of Independence" long before the Revolution, and their main enemies were the colonists who were now fighting for freedom from England.

One reason so many Americans were angry with England in the years before the Revolution was the British policy of protecting the right of Native Americans to keep their land.

King George III's Proclamation Line of 1763 prohibited colonists from settling beyond the Appalachian Mountains, where the "tribes of Indians" lived "under our protection," but the king's proclamation was largely ignored.

One speculator who ignored the proclamation and was determined to own some of their land was George Washington.

"I can never look upon that proclamation in any other light (but this I say between ourselves) than as a temporary expedient to quiet the minds of the Indians . . . ," he wrote in 1767, in asking a friend to survey a tract for him. "Any person therefore who neglects the present opportunity of hunting out good lands . . . will never regain it. . . ."

Thomas Jefferson felt the same way, and when the Revolutionary War began he saw an opportunity to seize traditional Cherokee lands.

By 1775, on the eve of the war, Washington and other whites owned thousands of acres of the Native Americans' prime farming, hunting, and fishing lands.

There was thus much anger toward American settlers, but most Native Americans tried to stay neutral once the war began. The powerful forces around them finally forced them to take sides, however, and most chose the British side (though Native Americans also fought in the Continental Army and aided it in other ways, such as giving food to the troops).

The result was brutal clashes in places that had been settled by whites over the objections of the Iroquois, including "massacres" (a word often used when whites were killed by Native Americans) in Wyoming Valley in eastern Pennsylvania and Cherry Valley in central New York.

The expedition of 1779 was meant to destroy the Iroquois as a sovereign nation, ending both their ability to make war and their ability to block American expansion onto their lands.

"The immediate objects are the total destruction of the hostile tribes of the Six Nations," Washington wrote to expedition leader General John Sullivan, "and the devastation of their settlements, and the capture of as many prisoners of every age and sex as possible."

The Iroquois had traditionally welcomed anyone who came in peace, including escaped slaves, who often married Iroquois women. Chief Thayendanegea of the Mohawks (Joseph Brant), who was educated at New Hampshire's Indian School — later Dartmouth College — was an especially strong believer in freedom for all people.

Now African Americans fought alongside Native Americans as Sullivan's troops invaded the land.

At one Iroquois town, said Lieutenant Erkuries Beatty, we "made more prisoners and killed some particularly a Negro who was their Dr. . . ."

Another soldier, coming on a town that had already been evacuated by the Iroquois, reported: "This place it is said was commanded by a negro, who was titled Capt. Sunfish, a very bold enterprising fellow."

The American army swept through the land of the Iroquois killing and scalping as they went. But the main effort of the soldiers was the destruction of every Iroquois home and food supply they could find.

They burned over 40 villages, including one with 122 houses which, according to one man, "were in an hour swept off by the torch."

Hundreds of Iroquois families starved in the long, harsh winter that followed, but their deaths did not make the survivors surrender. When spring finally arrived, Iroquois warriors came seeking revenge, more enraged than ever.

"Town Destroyer," the Iroquois called Washington, and in years to come used his name to frighten unruly children into behaving.

Even many colonists were appalled at the violence aimed at the Iroquois. Washington blamed Congress, and Sullivan, with no one to blame, resigned from the army. But first he received a gold medal and congratulations from Congress for his role in destroying the Six Nations.

The expedition into Iroquois territory had barely ended when Washington once more shifted his attention to the South. A combined French and American force was laying siege to Savannah, trying to wrest it from the British.

The leaders of South Carolina and Georgia still refused to arm slaves, so the army of General Benjamin Lincoln remained pathetically small: about 600 Continentals and 750 militiamen, plus the 200 cavalrymen under Count Pulaski.

Isom Carter, who described himself as "a free man of color descended from an Indian woman and a Negro man," was one of the men under Lincoln's command. Carter would eventually serve five years in the Continental Army, though he was constantly tormented by the fact that his "wife and children are slaves and have no one to support them."

The British force of 2,400 included many Loyalists from North and South Carolina, and about 200 escaped slaves. In the French ranks were 545 "Colored: Volunteer Chasseurs [troops trained and equipped to move rapidly] Mulattoes, and Negroes, newly raised at Santo Domingo" [present-day Haiti].

One of the black volunteers in this Fontages Legion, named after its French commander, was a twelve-year-old who would later fight for the independence of Haiti and be elected its first president: Henri Christophe.

Black fishermen guided hundreds of British reinforcements to Savannah, where they arrived under cover of a dense fog. These added troops, combined with the betrayal of the Allied plans by a deserting South Carolina militiaman, brought the Americans and French a crushing defeat: almost 1,100 dead and wounded, compared to British losses of less than 200.

The Allies might even have been annihilated if the Fontages Legion had not responded to the sudden British attack with "the most brilliant feat of the day," according to one man, thereby permitting an orderly American retreat.

A few days later, Count d'Estaing sailed away with the French force and Lincoln withdrew the shattered remnants of his army into the countryside.

Washington learned of the defeat at Savannah as he was preparing to move the Northern Army into winter quarters at Morristown, New Jersey. Though neither he nor his men yet knew it, the coming winter would be filled with mutiny, hunger, bitter cold, and death.

And once again the army seemed on the verge of disintegrating, with 8,000 enlistments due to expire by springtime out of the 10,000 to 12,000 men in camp.

But recruits continued to make their way into the ranks of the Continental Army despite the hardships and lack of pay. As usual, many of the recruits were African Americans.

From Plymouth, Massachusetts, came Primus Coburn, while William Jackson joined from Virginia and Cato Treadwell from Huntington, Connecticut. All three would serve for the remainder of the war.

And most black men who were already in the army decided to stay.

"I myself saw a battalion of them," said one white soldier, "as fine martial-looking men as I ever saw, attached to the Northern army."

In the months to come, the Patriot cause would need them all.

CHAPTER
8

As bad as Valley Forge had been two years before, the cold, hunger, and death at Morristown were even worse.

"The oldest people now living in this country do not remember so hard a winter," Washington told a friend.

In the first week of January 1780, howling blizzards piled drifts so deep they collapsed the men's ragged tents and hastily constructed huts.

Most of the soldiers ate the last of the meat they had been issued, and Washington was not even sure he could come up with three days' rations for a company that was supposed to go out on a special assignment.

"Poor fellows!" General Greene exclaimed. "A country overflowing with plenty are now suffering an Army, employed for the defence of everything that is dear and valuable, to perish for want of food."

The Continental Congress was controlled by the rich, and they concentrated more on the business needs of themselves and their friends than they did on feeding, clothing, and paying the soldiers. So while many wealthy men grew even richer, soldiers starved and a large part of the army "could not move on the most pressing exigency" because they had no shoes.

Soldiers began to roam the countryside and steal whatever food they could find. Washington issued orders to commandeer supplies from the local farmers and pay for it with Continental currency. This practice temporarily eased the threat of starvation, but aroused the anger of the inhabitants because the money continued to be almost worthless.

"We begin to hate the country for its neglect of us," wrote Alexander Hamilton. "The country begin to hate us for our oppressions of them."

A congressional committee visited Morristown and reported to their colleagues: "Their [the soldiers] starving condition, their want of pay, and the variety of hardships they have been driven to sustain, has soured their tempers and produced a spirit of discontent which begins to display itself under a complexion of the most alarming hue. . . ."

The hue became even more alarming one evening in May, when drums began to roll in the camps of the Fourth and Eighth Connecticut regiments, who had not received their allowance of meat for ten days.

"Growling like sore dogs," the men headed for the camp of two other Connecticut regiments to urge them

The
just man shall
be in eternal
remembrance

The brave Soldier
of the Revolutionary
War 1770.

Crispus Attucks, a fugitive slave, is considered by many to be the first person killed in the Revolutionary War. (Library of Congress)

Along with Crispus Attucks, four other men died in the Boston Massacre, one of the major clashes between the Patriots and British soldiers. (WPA/National Archives)

This painting of the Battle of Bunker Hill depicts Peter Salem shooting British Major John Pitcairn. (Negro History Association)

Lemuel Haynes received the first honorary degree of Master of Arts bestowed on an African American. (Schomburg Center for Research in Black Culture, New York Public Library)

On the night of April 19, 1775, Paul Revere made his famous ride, warning that the British were approaching Concord, Massachusetts.

Molly Pitcher took over her husband's position at a cannon when he was overcome by heat during the Battle of Monmouth, June 28, 1778. (Corbis-Bettmann)

Patrick Henry is best known for his stirring declaration, "Give me liberty or give me death." (Wide World)

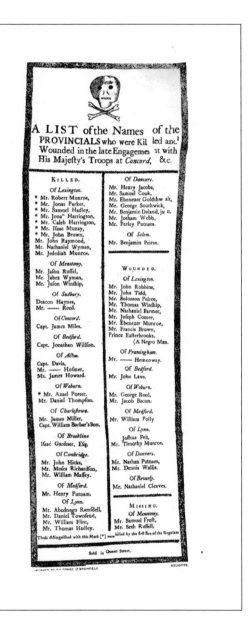

This list of patriots killed and wounded includes Prince Easterbrooks, "A Negro Man." (Rare Book Division, The New York Public Library, Astor, Lenox and Tilden Foundations)

Thomas Paine's essays on freedom rallied tens of thousands to the cause of American independence. (Library of Congress)

George Washington signed Oliver Cromwell's discharge, which honored him with the "Badge of Merit for Six Years faithful Service." (National Archives) to join a mutiny. Violence soon followed. A colonel was stabbed with a bayonet, while officers tried to bring the mutinous troops under control.

Finally a brigade of Pennsylvania soldiers surrounded the Connecticut regiments, and for awhile it seemed they would join them. Worried officers hurriedly conferred, then withdrew the Pennsylvanians and left the Connecticut troops to cool off on their own.

Washington now realized that the disgruntled, dwindling army would be too weak to do anything but act defensively in the coming campaign.

"I have almost ceased to hope," he said two days after the mutiny. And on May 31, after receiving word of a crushing British victory at Charleston, he declared that unless Congress and the states finally acted decisively to support the army, "Certain I am . . . that our cause is lost."

John Laurens declared that Charleston and South Carolina would have remained in American hands if his plan for enlisting slaves had been carried out.

The British quickly pushed into the interior of South Carolina, with Lieutenant Colonel Banastre Tarleton leading 270 mounted Loyalists. The Oxford-educated Tarleton's reputation for cold-blooded killing spread terror wherever he went and had earned him the nickname "Butcher."

On May 29, in a region known as the Waxhaws, he forced the surrender of almost 400 Patriots. Tarleton then proceeded to butcher most of them on the pretext that some had fired after they surrendered.

Knowledge of the "Massacre of the Waxhaws" spread like wildfire throughout North and South Carolina, and helped convert many previously neutral Americans to the Patriot cause. It would also lead to savage reprisals in the months to come.

Thousands of South Carolina slaves fled to the British in the wake of their capture of Charleston.

Young British Major John André wrote Clinton about the massive number of runaways and their destructive impact on the Patriot cause: "Their property [slaves] we need not seek," he said, "it flys to us and famine follows."

American naval commanders responded by seizing slaves from Loyalist plantations at every opportunity.

In one raid on Virginia's island-fringed coast, an American privateer carried off 8 slaves from their Loyalist owner, while a British sympathizer on the Savannah River lost 15 "working" slaves and 7 children to another privateer.

Several hours before dawn on August 16, an American force of approximately 1,000 Continental veterans and 2,000 North Carolina and Virginia militia, accidentally bumped into a much larger British force in a pine forest near Camden, South Carolina.

Three of the Continental Army soldiers who quickly

prepared to do battle in the sultry darkness were black veterans Andrew Ferguson and Ambrose Lewis of Virginia and Record Primes of North Carolina.

At dawn the British, under Cornwallis, charged the Virginia militia with fixed bayonets. Artillery blazed from both sides on the windless morning and gunsmoke mingling with haze clung low to the ground.

The inexperienced Virginians, who were holding the right side of the American line, fired a few wild shots, then threw down their muskets and fled.

The panic-stricken militia from North Carolina soon followed, melting away the center of the American line. By now 2,500 Americans were streaming backwards "like an undamned torrent . . . raving along the roads and byways toward the north."

The Americans, who were commanded by General Horatio Gates, lost over 1,000 men killed and wounded at the Battle of Camden, and an unknown number captured.

The British reported their losses at 324, but the figure may have been twice as high.

Ambrose Lewis, who was shot through the thigh with a musket ball and received severe bayonet slashes in his arms, legs, and torso, was captured and imprisoned for the rest of the war.

Andrew Ferguson, wounded in the head and leg, was also captured, but would soon manage to escape. Record Primes was wounded in the head, but eluded his pursuers and was ready to fight the British again less than two months later.

General Gates fled north so fast he reached Charlotte, sixty miles away, that same night. Two days later he was in Hillsboro, 180 miles from the battlefield.

A disgusted Alexander Hamilton commented drily on the speed and distance covered by Gates, asking: "But was there ever an instance of a general running away . . . from his whole army? And was there ever so precipitous a flight? One hundred and eighty miles in three days and a half! It does admirable credit to the activity of a man at his time of life. . . ."

No sooner had Washington received word of Gates' disaster at Camden, than he was struck with an even greater calamity: the discovery that Benedict Arnold, commander of West Point and one of Washington's most trusted generals, was a traitor.

For more than 15 months, Arnold had been secretly corresponding with Clinton about handing over West Point. The fortress — called "the key to America" — stood guard over the Hudson River and the waterway highway it controlled, from New York City in the south to Canada in the north.

Washington had been puzzled by the energetic Arnold's request to be placed in such an inactive command, and had originally turned him down.

In return for Arnold's betrayal of West Point, along

with its 3,000 soldiers and vast military stores, he was promised £20,000 in gold and a general's commission in the British army.

Early one morning in September 1780, Major John André was rowed ashore from the British warship HMS *Vulture* to make final arrangements with Arnold. They met in a woods several miles below West Point (not far from the site of Anthony Wayne's victory at Stony Point), and Arnold handed over detailed plans of the fort.

He then set off for West Point to await an inspection visit from Washington, while André prepared to return to the *Vulture*. But as André made his way to the ship, he suddenly heard cannon fire and saw the *Vulture* taking hits that damaged its rigging.

Years later, the obituary of John Peterson, the black soldier who had fought at Saratoga, told the story of what had happened next.

Peterson and a friend named Moses Sherwood "were engaged in making cider, at Barrett's farm . . . they had taken their arms with them. . . . [Moses Sherwood] saw a barge filled with armed men from the *Vulture*, in company with a gun-boat, approaching the shore. . . ."

Peterson and Sherwood fired at the barge, hitting at least one man and forcing the sailors "to return to the *Vulture* . . . Many [armed townsmen] now . . . opened a well-directed fire on the *Vulture*. . . ."

André saw the warship "slip her cable and make sail for New York. . . . But for the firing of Peterson and Sherwood upon the barge, it is more than probable he [André] would have returned to the *Vulture* in safety."

Trying to escape to New York City on horseback, André was captured wearing civilian clothes, despite Clinton's warning to always wear his uniform. By dressing as a civilian, André could be hanged as a spy.

The papers he had hidden in his boots were delivered to Washington, who cried out in despair: "Arnold has betrayed us! . . . Whom can we trust now?"

At noon on October 2, André was led to the top of a hill where a gallows had been built.

"Must I die then in this manner?" he asked, drawing back. Then he strode forward, mounted the steps and was hanged while the watching crowd yelled and moaned.

Peterson was awarded a pension by the United States government for his actions, and New York's Colonel Philip Van Cortlandt gave him a house.

Washington, realizing that Arnold had deliberately weakened the fortifications at West Point, quickly gave orders to have them strengthened. He also began making plans for the disposition of his army for the coming fall and winter.

The states had promised him 16,500 new recruits, but only about 6,000 showed up. It was also clear that the British were going to try and extend their conquests in the South, where General Nathanael Greene had been named to replace the disgraced Gates.

With their victories at Charleston and Camden, the British now controlled Georgia and South Carolina. General Clinton and Lord Cornwallis moved quickly to expand that control into North Carolina, as the next step in conquering the entire South.

Cornwallis pushed toward North Carolina, his left flank screened by a force of over 1,100 Loyalist militiamen and rangers, mostly from South Carolina. They were led by Major Patrick Ferguson, a British officer from Scotland whose troops called him "the Bulldog."

Frontiersmen from the Carolina mountains had tried to stay neutral in the war, feeling the Patriot side was being run by the same rich men who had made their lives miserable with unfair laws and taxes before the Revolution.

Now, however, the murders in the Waxhaws and other places had driven them over to the Patriots, and they rallied by the hundreds to try and stop Ferguson as he marched through the northern part of South Carolina.

The two sides met at a rocky spur of the Blue Ridge Mountains that was about a mile long and 300 yards wide near the border with North Carolina: King's Mountain.

Most of the men on both sides were Americans,

and many knew each other. Several months before, at Ramsour's Mill in North Carolina, there had been a similar battle of Americans against Americans.

Eight hundred Loyalists and Patriots, about equally divided, had gone at each other. When they ran out of gunpowder, they used clubs. By the time the battle was over, almost 300 men lay dead.

The Battle of King's Mountain on October 7, 1780, would be just as brutal.

The Patriots were within a quarter mile of the top before Ferguson's men knew they were coming up the steep, forested slopes. Mounted on a white horse, waving a sword, and blowing a silver whistle to signal his men, the British major led four bayonet charges that drove the Patriots back. Each time, however, sharpshooters mowed down more of his men.

On the fifth charge, Ferguson was killed as seven shots ripped through his body and dozens of others literally tore apart his clothes.

While Ferguson's body hung by one stirrup from his white horse, the Patriots drove his panic-stricken men "along the summit" reported Colonel William Campbell of the Virginia militia, "nearly to the other end, where they huddled in the greatest confusion: the flag for a surrender was immediately hoisted. . . ."

But many of the Patriots were in no mood to honor a flag of surrender, or the white handkerchiefs that scores of desperate Loyalists now waved from the ends of their bayonets.

The battle had lasted one hour. Now, with cries of "Tarleton's quarter!" filling the air, the cold-blooded killing began. Patriots thirsting for revenge for the murder of family and friends, singled out Loyalist neighbors and shot, stabbed, or clubbed them down. Colonel Campbell had commanded his men to fire at the prisoners, but finally was sickened by the slaughter and yelled, "For God's sake, quit! It's murder to shoot anymore!"

Except for 200 men who were off foraging for food when the battle began, all of Ferguson's troops were killed, wounded, or captured. The Patriot loss was only 90 killed and wounded. Nine prisoners were hanged the next day after a trial that found them guilty of helping the British raid, loot, and burn Patriot homes in the Carolinas.

The same day, remembered James Collins, who lived nearby and fought as a sixteen-year-old militiaman alongside his father, "The wives and children of the poor Tories came in, in great numbers. Their husbands, fathers and brothers lay dead in heaps, while others lay wounded or dying. . . ."

Most of the dead were buried under partially exposed coverings of rocks, logs, or bark that wild animals would soon find. In the weeks to come "the wolves became so plenty, that it was dangerous for anyone to be out at night . . . ," declared Collins.

Clinton called the American victory at King's Mountain "the first link in a chain of evils that followed each other in regular succession until they at last ended in the total loss of America."

Most of the Patriot militiamen went back home after King's Mountain, but the tales of horror that survivors told frightened many Loyalists into silence or reluctant support of the American cause.

"It seemed like a calm after a heavy storm," said the young Collins, ". . . and for a short time, every man could visit his home, or his neighbor without being afraid. . . ."

But it was a brief calm, for Washington and the Continental Army were more destitute than ever. General Greene begged for support as he made his way to take command of the Southern Army, but he received pitifully little in either men or supplies.

When Greene arrived at Charlotte, North Carolina, in early December, he found that his army consisted of a little over 2,300 soldiers on paper, but that fewer than 1,500 were actually present. Of these, just 949 were Continentals and the rest were militia. All were on starvation rations and only 800 men were properly equipped and clothed.

The hungry soldiers were "so addicted to plundering," he said, "that they were a terror to the inhabitants." Greene ordered one man hanged for stealing food and forced his comrades to watch.

Washington sent one of his favorite commanders to reinforce Greene: Captain Henry ("Light-Horse Harry") Lee, with his legion of 100 cavalrymen and 180 infantrymen.

But the officially-named Grand Army of the Southern Department of the United States of America, Greene concluded sadly, was "rather a shadow than a substance, having merely an imaginary existence."

"What a Herculean task we have," he wrote Lafayette, "to contend with a formidable enemy with a handful of men."

The logical answer to the army's manpower shortage, Greene decided, was the same one John Laurens had come up with: Enlist slaves and give them their freedom.

"That they would make good soldiers, I have not the least doubt," he wrote Governor Rutledge of South Carolina.

Instead of following Greene's suggestion, however, General Thomas Sumter of South Carolina offered slave bonuses to any white man who would join. Sumter based his bonuses on the enlistee's rank, starting with one adult slave for a private and going all the way up to three adults and one child for a colonel.

The Virginia legislature, with Jefferson presiding, voted to give every new recruit his choice of a slave between the ages of ten and thirty, or £60 in gold or silver.

Liberating the slaves and arming them, said James Madison when he heard of these plans, "would certainly be more consonant to the principles of liberty, which ought never to be lost sight of in a contest for liberty."

But despite his agreement with Madison that the slaves should be freed and armed, General Greene permitted Sumter to use slaves from a Loyalist plantation as "down payments" for new recruits.

With so many slaves running away, however, there must have been few to spare. Soon the men in one regiment were owed 74 out of a promised 120 slaves. And the men in the regiment of South Carolina's General Wade Hampton, said to be the wealthiest planter/slave owner in America, were somehow owed ninety-three and three-quarters adults and "Three Quarters of a Small Negro."

The South Carolina legislature authorized the governor to deliver 460 slaves to various regiments in order to meet their back pay obligations.

Even with the lure of slave bonuses, however, few whites joined the Southern Army and Washington, with problems of his own, could send Greene no more troops.

The dejected commander in chief led his men into winter quarters in camps stretching from West Point to Morristown, "drawing an inactive campaign to a close. . . . We have lived upon expedients till we can live no longer," he wrote Congress. "In a word, the history of the war is a history of false hopes. . . ."

The unpaid, ragged, and hungry men in his army also thought the war was filled with false hopes — false hopes they were tired of enduring.

Congress and the public seemed to have forgotten them, while both officers and civilians who had not risked their lives grew rich from their suffering.

"Eighteen generals quit," said Major Tallmadge, director of the Continental Army's secret service, "many out of pique, some to escape arrest for taking double pay."

Many of the surgeons, declared Washington, "are great rascals . . . often receiving bribes to certify indispositions and drawing medicines . . . for private purposes."

As the cold days of January 1781 began, thousands of angry soldiers discovered that new troops, including convicts promised freedom for enlisting, were to receive bonuses of money and land while battle-hardened veterans continued to go unpaid.

Their anger was about to explode, and Washington foresaw both the causes and the consequences.

"Instead of having Magazines filled with provisions, we have a scanty pittance scattered here and there . . . ," he complained to Congress. "Instead of having our

Arsenals well supplied with Military Stores, they are poorly provided, and the Workmen all leaving them. . . . In a word — instead of having everything . . . we have nothing. . . ."

And soon, he declared, "We shall have no men, [even] if we had money to pay them."

A great number of men deserted every day, according to one observer.

"Yesterday three men belonging to the Maryland line were found going to the enemy . . . ," he wrote. "The one was shot and his head cut off and this morning was brought to the Virginia Camp and put on top of the gallows of a man who was executed and hung."

The desertion rate among black soldiers continued to be low, however, perhaps because they were beginning to see a little progress in the status of black Americans in general, at least in the North.

Wentworth Cheswill, who had fought at Saratoga, was elected by voters in his hometown of Newmarket, New Hampshire, as a delegate to help draw up the state constitution. They also chose him to be a town selectman.

A large part of the growing willingness of black Americans to speak out against inequality, came from the knowledge that black men were doing so much of the fighting and dying.

Brothers Paul and John Cuffee of Dartmouth,

Massachusetts (both successful merchants), protesting that African American residents were denied the right to vote even though they paid taxes, declared "that their is more of our Colour gone into the wars according to the Number of them into the Respepiktive towns than any other nation here. . . ."

Now even more of that large "Number" were about to go "into the wars" in the climactic year of the struggle for independence: 1781. They would suffer much, and the army would once again be torn by mutiny.

Before the year was out, however, these black soldiers and their white comrades would do much to help lay the foundation of the new nation.

Their most important actions would come at a small tobacco trading port in Virginia most of them had never heard of: Yorktown.

CHAPTER
9

The three-year enlistments of most of the veterans in the Pennsylvania regiments were due to expire January 1, 1781, but they were not sure they would be discharged as promised. In addition, like the majority of Continental Army soldiers, they had not been paid for months.

Then, when they learned that new recruits were being given 81 dollars in silver and a promise of 200 acres of land after the war, the anger of the veterans exploded.

On New Year's Day, shouting and firing muskets and cannon, they headed for Philadelphia to confront members of the Continental Congress.

Anthony Wayne was celebrating the holiday when he was informed of the mutiny. Leaping on his horse, he raced after the soldiers and begged them to stop, but they were in no mood to listen. Wayne blocked their way, tore open his coat, and dared the mutineers to shoot him if they wanted to continue. They refused, saying their quarrel was with Congress, not him. Then they resumed their march.

A widespread mutiny of the army had been one of Washington's greatest fears since the war began. Now he was filled "with extreme anxiety and pain of mind" as to how far the mutiny would go and what he should do about it.

He knew the only permanent solution to the soldiers' anger was to give them adequate food and pay. He also knew that the only possible sources for that were the New England states, and so he appealed to them for help.

"At what point this defection will stop, or how extensive it may prove, God only knows," Washington wrote President Meshech Weare of New Hampshire four days after the mutiny began. "At present the troops at the important posts in this vicinity remain quiet . . . but how long they will remain so, cannot be ascertained. . . ."

The soldiers elected a Board of Sergeants to negotiate with Joseph Reed, the president of Pennsylvania. Reed ended the mutiny by promising to give the soldiers at least part of their back pay, and to grant discharges to more than 1,300 of them. An additional several hundred were promised furloughs in a few weeks.

No sooner had the mutiny of the Pennsylvania regiments ended, however, than three regiments from New Jersey mutinied. This time Washington reacted harshly, ordering General Robert Howe to choose up to six hundred of the "most robust and best clothed" men he had and "compel the mutineers to unconditional surrender. . . . You will instantly execute a few of the most active and incendiary leaders."

The men Howe chose were all from Massachusetts regiments. They surrounded the cabins of the sleeping mutineers at night, trained artillery on them, and set a deadline of five minutes for their surrender. Just before the deadline was up, men began stumbling from their cabins, wrapped in tattered blankets to guard against the cold.

One man was chosen from each regiment and sentenced to die. Their weeping, protesting comrades were forced to kill two of them, and the third was granted a reprieve when his officers said he had tried to stop the mutiny.

"We have reason to believe the mutinous disposition of the troops is now completely subdued," Washington wrote Congress that afternoon, "and succeeded by a genuine penitence."

In the midst of these troubles, he received news from General Greene of an unexpected American victory over one of their most hated foes: Banastre "Butcher" Tarleton.

As poorly supplied as he was with food, Greene knew his Southern Army could survive only if they lived off the land. He therefore took perhaps the greatest chance of any commander in the war, and weakened the small army even further by dividing it in half.

Greene kept command of one division and placed the other under Brigadier General Daniel Morgan. Uncertain what Greene was up to, Cornwallis also divided his army. It was a mistake that would eventually prove fatal.

He sent Tarleton chasing after Morgan, and the rash, young officer caught up with the Virginia commander in a clearing where cattle wandered in open cowpens among low, sandy hills. Situated near present-day Spartanburg, South Carolina, by a bend in the Broad River, the area was called "the Cowpens."

Both sides had about 1,100 men, but most of Tarleton's were trained regulars, including his dreaded 400-men cavalry and infantry legion. Militiamen comprised the majority of Morgan's force, but he also commanded about 400 Continental veterans of de Kalb's defeated army.

Record Primes was ready to do battle again after receiving the head wound at Camden and suffering the horrors of King's Mountain. One of the many other black soldiers awaiting Tarleton's onslaught at the Cowpens was Fortune Freeman, veteran of

Brandywine, Monmouth (where he was shot in the thigh), and Saratoga.

One of the American heroes was a young black bugler "too small to wield a sword." When Colonel William Washington was about to be cut down by a British officer, the bugler wounded the officer "with a ball from a pistol."

The Battle of Cowpens lasted almost two hours, and when it was over Tarleton's force was shattered. He and his men fled for twenty miles before escaping, pausing only long enough to hack to death several Americans they found carrying off British supplies.

Tarleton reportedly lay on the ground all night without uttering a word, so humiliated was he by his devastating defeat.

He lost over 300 men killed and wounded, and over 600 taken prisoner.

One captured British officer said the defeat should have been expected because Tarleton was "a foolish boy."

Morgan's forces also captured wagons, cannons, horses, and about 60 slaves who had escaped to the British. There is no record of what was done with the captured slaves, but they were probably sold or forced to work as laborers for the American army.

Patriot losses at Cowpens were only 12 killed and 60 wounded.

Twenty-four hours after the battle, Cornwallis started chasing Morgan, burning most of his army's huge, cumbersome baggage train in a desperate attempt to catch the fast-traveling, lightly equipped Americans.

Greene quickly reached Morgan and reunited the two armies. For the next several weeks he kept just ahead of Cornwallis, purposely leading him farther and farther from the British supply base in South Carolina.

At one river where Greene's forces ambushed the British as they struggled through swirling water weighed down by heavy knapsacks, a local inhabitant said of the Redcoats: "The river was full of 'em, a-snortin' and a-hollerin' and a-drownin'."

The American general hoped to wear down the British army while he strengthened his own, and he succeeded. On March 15, with the British army so weakened by sickness, hunger, and desertions that it numbered less than 2,000, and with the American army grown to 4,400 strong, Greene turned to fight at Guilford Courthouse in North Carolina.

Greene used the same tactic Morgan had used at Cowpens, knowing that sooner or later the raw militiamen among his troops would break and run.

"Two rounds, my boys," he told them, "and then you may fall back."

Backing up the militia and expected to do most of

the fighting were the Continental troops, numbering almost 1,800 infantry and cavalry. There were also several hundred experienced sharpshooter militiamen.

Record Primes and Andrew Ferguson were ready to fight again. And about to engage in his first battle was a free black man named Mathew Williams, a native of Southampton, Virginia, who had recently joined Colonel Dabney's Virginia regiment.

At about 1:30 P.M. on March 15, 1781, the British began their advance. The militiamen fired one volley. Then, seeing rows of bayonets bearing down on them, most of them turned and ran without waiting to fire a second shot.

At one point, Cornwallis even ordered his artillery to fire grapeshot into a mass of struggling British and American soldiers in order to stop the American advance. Some of his officers protested and turned away sick at the sight of their men being killed and mangled by their own guns.

Again and again, though, Cornwallis ordered the artillery to fire away. The tactic was brutal but effective, and sent the Continentals reeling backward.

By then all of Greene's militia had run away and many of the Continentals were scattered across the battlefield. Faced with the danger of losing his army, Greene ordered a retreat. But it was a hollow victory for the British, costing Cornwallis a third of his army, including three generals and 26 other officers killed or wounded.

American losses were only 78 dead and 183 wounded. Mathew Williams was one of the wounded, shot in the knee by a musket ball.

In the first three months of 1781, Greene and his valiant army had turned the tide of the war, but neither he nor Washington realized this. On the contrary, both were painfully aware that the Patriot cause could still meet with defeat.

"The whole country is in danger of being laid waste," Greene wrote Congress, "by the Whigs and Tories who pursue each other with as relentless fury as beasts of prey."

Greene would fight three more battles against the British in the months to come, including one at Eutaw Springs, South Carolina.

James Nickens, whose Virginia family had sent so many members to fight for the Patriot cause, was one of many African American soldiers at Eutaw Springs.

Most came through the battle unscathed, but one of their colleagues whose name has been lost to history was not so lucky. Survivors were startled when they came upon a black American soldier and a British soldier, each impaled on the other's bayonet.

Over 700 men were wounded in the battle, divided almost equally between Americans and British. Agrippa

Hull, the black veteran from Massachusetts who had fought at Saratoga, helped the surgeons with their gory work. Though he lived to be eighty-nine years old, Hull said he never forgot the horror of the bloody amputations at Eutaw Springs that day.

Greene lost each of the battles he fought, but always ended up in better shape than Cornwallis, who saw his army steadily shrink and his supply lines grow longer.

"There are few generals that has run oftener, or more lustily, than I have done," Greene wrote. "But I have taken care not to run too far, and commonly have run as fast forward as backward. . . ."

In the North, Washington agonized over how best to help Greene while still protecting himself against General Clinton's forces in New York City. He had already dispatched Lafayette to Virginia with 2,300 Continentals to try to defend it against Cornwallis and Benedict Arnold, who was now a brigadier general in the British army.

But the twenty-three-year-old Lafayette found himself so outnumbered, he wrote Washington, "I am not strong enough even to get beaten."

Lafayette knew that if his army was to move swiftly enough to effectively harass Cornwallis and Arnold, he had to somehow find enough horses to mount a large cavalry. The only hope Lafayette saw for this was in convincing black men to assist the army or, as he wrote Washington: "Nothing but a treaty of alliance with the

Negroes can find us dragoon Horses, and it is by this the enemy have so formidable a Cavalry."

Lafayette asked Jefferson for 400 black laborers and wagoners, but only a handful of Virginia's slave owners agreed to lend their slaves to the Patriot cause.

Lafayette's thoughts also turned to black men when it came to that most dangerous wartime task of all: spying. Sudden death awaited spies, but Lafayette quickly recruited a man he would remember and praise for the rest of his life.

James Armistead was a twenty-one-year-old black man held as a slave on a farm near Williamsburg, and even though he was promised nothing in return, he willingly risked his life for Lafayette and the cause of American independence.

Armistead went to Benedict Arnold's camp and worked as a volunteer, listening quietly to the officers as they talked among themselves. Then he used other black men as messengers to take his reports back to Lafayette on an almost daily basis, or made the journey himself.

"Often at the peril of his life," read a petition approved by the Virginia Assembly years later, Armistead "kept open a channel of the most useful information to the army of the state . . . of the most secret & important kind. . . ."

When Arnold was transferred to New York, Armistead went into the camp of Cornwallis at

Portsmouth, Virginia, and spied on him, even managing to work in the tent of the unsuspecting general.

Armistead was so good at not attracting suspicion that Cornwallis hired him to spy on Lafayette, a fact Armistead quickly reported to the French general.

But Cornwallis was so cautious with his maps and plans that Armistead found it hard to see them.

"His Lordship is so shy of his papers," Lafayette wrote Washington, "that my honest friend says he cannot get at them."

Lafayette continued to keep his forces near Cornwallis, though, and Armistead was able to warn him of British moves within hours. Cornwallis seldom even knew that "the boy" (as he called Lafayette) was shadowing him just a few miles behind, using a black spy to keep watch over a foe the Americans were too weak to defeat.

"He perfectly acquitted himself," Lafayette remembered years later of Armistead's spying, adding: "His intelligence from the enemy's camps were industriously collected and more faithfully delivered. . . ."

Another black spy in Virginia at this time was Saul Mathews, who was a private in the army. Mathews risked his life to go into British garrisons and carry back information about plans and troop movements.

His work was so vital to the American cause that Colonel Josiah Parker of the Virginia militia said he deserved the applause of his country. The African-

American spy was also praised by Lafayette, Baron von Steuben, General Greene, and Colonel Peter Muhlenburg, a brigade commander in Greene's army.

There was not much action in the North now, but on May 13, 1781, a British-led Loyalist force attacked the American lines near a ford in the Croton River, several miles above New York City. Their troops drove directly at the headquarters of Colonel Christopher Greene of the Black Regiment of Rhode Island.

In the action that followed, wrote one man, "Colonel Greene . . . was cut down and mortally wounded; but the sabres of the enemy only reached him through the bodies of his faithful guard of blacks, who hovered over him to protect him, *and every one of whom was killed.*"

One hundred other members of the regiment were wounded and 30 taken prisoner. Most of the prisoners were sold into slavery in the British West Indies.

The soldiers who were killed were buried near where they fell, the black men in one grave and their white officers in another. The bodies of these Revolutionary soldiers still lie beneath separate stone memorials alongside a church in the quiet New York countryside.

At the end of May, Washington informed Lafayette that he was going to conduct a joint operation with the French against New York City.

The plan would make the British withdraw part of their force from the South and would also, if successful,

result in the rescue of the thousands of Americans being held on British prison ships in New York Harbor.
Approximately 11,500 would die during the war in the
dark, cramped, disease-ridden holds where men froze
in the winter and sweltered in the summer.

In the holds of the *Jersey*, said Captain Thomas
Drinig, who was imprisoned there for nine months, the
seamen were "taught the utmost extent of human
misery."

One of the prisoners was a black fifteen-year-old
named James Forten. Forten had served on the *Royal
Louis*, a privateer that was captured on its second
cruise by the British warship *Amphyon*. Twenty of the
American ship's crew of a hundred were black, and
most of them were sold into slavery in the West Indies.

Forten became such good friends with the British
captain's young son, however, that the captain offered
Forten a life of privilege in England if he would re-
nounce his allegiance to the United States.

"I am here a prisoner for the liberties of my country,"
Forten replied. "I never, never, shall prove a traitor to
her interests!"

The youth was then transferred to the *Jersey*, where
the resourceful lad quickly came up with a plan to escape by hiding in a "chest of old clothes" that would
soon be carried ashore.

At the last minute, however, he gave up his place to
an even younger prisoner and even helped carry the

chest containing the concealed youth down the gang-plank.

John Peterson, the black veteran who had helped drive away the *Vulture* when it came to pick up Major André, had also been a prisoner on the *Jersey* for several months before escaping by climbing down the anchor chain.

As the summer of 1781 arrived, Washington continued to make plans to capture New York City with the help of the French. But Count Jean Baptiste de Rochambeau, commander of the French force, felt that an attack against the strongly entrenched British would be disastrous. Instead, he told Washington, their combined forces should move south to help Lafayette in Virginia.

"I will not conceal from you, Monsieur," he wrote French Admiral Count François de Grasse, in urging him to bring troops, ships and money as quickly as possible, "that the Americans are at the end of their resources, that Washington will not have half of the troops he is reckoned to have, and that . . . at present he does not have 6,000 men."

The French forces of Rochambeau joined the Continental Army at White Plains, and saw the tattered Americans for the first time.

"It was really painful to see these brave men," wrote Baron Ludwig von Closen, Rochambeau's aide-de-camp, "almost naked, with only some trousers and little linen jackets, most of them without stockings, but, believe it or not, very cheerful and healthy in appearance. A quarter of them were Negroes, merry, confident, and sturdy."

In late July, screened by 5,000 soldiers, Washington and Rochambeau made a reconnaissance of the British defenses in New York City. When he saw the powerful fortifications the British had built, Washington finally gave up on his plan to storm the city.

Rochambeau continued to urge him to move their forces south, but Washington seemed indecisive. He still had trouble feeding and clothing his army (though the French were about to provide the necessary money), and the states had delivered only about half the troops they had promised.

Then suddenly, without warning, events moved with a swiftness that must have startled Washington.

He had asked Lafayette to keep him informed of Cornwallis's plans and military strength, but Lafayette was able to learn nothing until Armistead finally contacted him.

"A correspondent of mine [Armistead] . . . writes on the 26th of July at Portsmouth," Lafayette told Washington, "and says . . . the greatest part of the army is embarked. There is in Hampton Road one 50 guns ship . . . 18 sloop loaded with horses. There remain but nine vessels in Portsmouth. . . ."

Armistead's information led Lafayette to suggest that if a French fleet quickly entered Hampton Roads at the entrance to Chesapeake Bay, the British army might be trapped.

Two weeks later, Washington received word that Admiral de Grasse was already on his way to Chesapeake Bay with a powerful force of warships and soldiers. He could only stay on the American coast until the middle of October, though, French officials warned.

This powerful fleet was just what the Americans needed, and Washington immediately sent word to Lafayette. Stop Cornwallis from leaving Virginia, he ordered. Washington also wrote to de Grasse, arranging a rendezvous with him in the Chesapeake Bay for operations against the British in either Virginia or South Carolina.

Within days, the American and French armies began moving south from New York City, still uncertain of their exact destination. And then suddenly another urgent message arrived from Lafayette.

At first, Armistead had been unable to discover where the British had gone once they left Portsmouth. Now he knew.

"I have got some intelligences by way of this servant [Armistead] I have mentioned . . . ," Lafayette wrote Washington. "I hear that they begin fortifying at York. . . . The enemy have 60 sails of vessels into York

River. . . . In a word this part affords the greatest number of regulars and the only active Army to attak [sic]."

At last Washington and Rochambeau knew where to strike: at the village of Yorktown.

Yorktown was on the tip of a peninsula, surrounded on three sides by water and swamps. Cornwallis had put himself in a perfect trap, if only reinforcements could arrive in time to spring the trap.

Not knowing that de Grasse was coming with his powerful fleet, the British commander expected the Royal Navy to keep the sea lanes open for reinforcements from New York.

With only Lafayette's small army of Continentals and Virginia militia blocking the way, Cornwallis slowly began fortifying his trap instead of trying to fight his way back out.

Admiral de Grasse's mighty fleet was already nearing Yorktown, and the eight ships of French Admiral Comte de Barras would soon head there also, carrying heavy siege guns.

". . . in a word," Washington had written John Laurens several weeks before, "we are at the end of our tether and now or never our deliverance must come."

If all went well in the campaign that was about to begin, the new nation's deliverance would come now.

CHAPTER
10

Rochambeau had given orders for the French in New Jersey to build barracks and bread ovens "to make Clinton believe that the army would remain encamped in that region."

The American and French soldiers then began marching toward the new facilities as the British watched from a distance.

Suddenly, on August 30, the soldiers turned south and the race to Yorktown was on. It took Clinton almost a week to realize that fact, however, and by then it was too late.

The line of allied soldiers stretched for two miles, said army surgeon James Thacher, and was followed by "a great number of wagons, loaded with tents, provisions and other baggage, such as a few soldiers' wives and children, though a very small number of these were allowed to encumber us on this occasion."

De Grasse arrived in Chesapeake Bay the first week

in September with 28 warships, 13,000 sailors, and 3,500 troops. He immediately put the troops ashore so they could strengthen Lafayette's army.

No sooner had this been done than 19 British ships sailed toward the main entrance to Chesapeake Bay, hoping to trap the French.

The French were able to escape, however, led by de Grasse aboard his huge 110-gun *Ville de Paris*, the mightiest naval vessel of its time.

Miles out at sea, the two sides began a running, two-hour fight, firing broadside after broadside that could be heard onshore. One British ship, the HMS *Terrible*, was so badly damaged it was abandoned and blown up.

By nightfall 350 British seamen had been killed, and "many English ships . . . navigated along, some without a main top, some without a bowsprit, some without a fore-top mast."

Then a fierce storm blew up, battering the British fleet even more. A few days later the ships sailed to New York for repairs.

Chesapeake Bay was now controlled by the French, cutting Cornwallis off from help by way of the sea, while on the land Lafayette's blockading army had been reinforced by 3,200 Virginia militiamen.

The British commander, who did not know the outcome of the huge naval battle miles out at sea, continued to build the extensive fortifications he thought would protect him until Clinton arrived with reinforcements.

Clinton's only action at this time, however, was to send Benedict Arnold on a raid to Connecticut. Leading a force of British regulars, Hessians, and Loyalists, Arnold burned 140 houses to the ground in New London and Groton, and captured Forts Trumbull and Griswold.

Major William Montgomery, the British commander in charge of the assault on Fort Griswold, tried to scale a wall and was killed by spears in the hands of a white officer and a black Connecticut militiaman named Jordan Freeman.

Another black militiaman, whose name was Lambert Latham, also distinguished himself at Fort Griswold, "loading and discharging his musket with great rapidity, even after he had been severely wounded in one of his hands."

When the British forced their way into the fort, the surrendering American commander handed his sword to a British officer. The officer promptly used it to kill the American, Lieutenant Colonel William Ledyard.

Latham leaped on the British officer and ran his bayonet through him. Within seconds, Latham lay dead from thirty-three bayonet wounds inflicted by enraged British soldiers.

The defenseless Patriot captives were then bayonetted

as they pleaded for mercy or tried to hide. By the time the slaughter was over, 85 of the defenders lay dead, 60 were wounded and 70 had been taken prisoner.

Almost fifty years later, a granite shaft was erected near the site "in memory of the brave patriots who fell in the massacre at Fort Griswold. . . ."

The names of the two black patriots were placed at the bottom, separated from the names of their white comrades by the label "Colored men."

A nineteenth-century abolitionist named Parker Pillsbury, noting that Jordan Freeman's name came "last on the list of heroes," called him "perhaps the greatest hero of them all."

While the raids at New London and Groton were taking place, the allied armies were nearing Baltimore. Twelve members of a Pennsylvania regiment persuaded other soldiers not to go any farther until they were paid.

General Wayne tried to talk the men into continuing, but they refused. A platoon then opened fire at Wayne's command, killing six of the leaders. Five other mutineers were hanged.

On the evening of September 28, the armies arrived at Yorktown: 8,800 Continentals and 7,800 French, plus several regiments of Virginia militia.

Cornwallis had turned the village into a fortress, with deep trenches, artillery batteries, and strong redoubts (small forts) guarding the approaches.

Patriot soldiers prepared to follow Washington's orders "to place their principle reliance on the Bayonet, that they may prove the Vanity of the Boast which the British make of their particular prowess in deciding Battles with that Weapon."

William Flora stood before Yorktown, still wielding the musket he had used against the British with such devastating accuracy at the Battle of Great Bridge six years before.

Oliver Cromwell was there, the veteran who had crossed the Delaware with Washington and gone on to fight at Trenton, Princeton, Brandywine, and Monmouth.

Fortune Freeman of Massachusetts was there, along with the veterans Record Primes of North Carolina and Thomas Lively of Virginia. Agrippa Hull, now an orderly for Count Tadeusz Kosciuszko, was by the young nobleman's side as they stood before Yorktown.

And as impressive as any Continental Army unit preparing for the decisive battle of the war, was the Black Regiment of Rhode Island — its veterans still grieving over the loss of Colonel Greene and their comrades at Points Bridge.

The Americans and French began to slowly tighten the noose around Cornwallis and his army, forcing them to retreat into an ever-smaller area.

The British used hundreds of slaves to help build

their fortifications, and they fell victim to both small-pox and the horrendous artillery fire.

"An immense number of Negroes have died, in the most miserable manner, in York," said one observer.

Cornwallis also forced out slaves he could no longer use or feed, and one soldier said they "might be seen scattered about in every direction" with "the smallpox for their bounty and starvation and death for their wages."

The toll on the British was so high that many deserted and even Cornwallis was forced to take refuge in a cave.

"We continue to lose men very fast," he wrote Clinton, who had still not left New York.

On October 12 the Americans and French opened a second parallel line, this time "300 yards in front of the first, and 300 yards from the enemy's works. . . ."

Then they moved up the siege guns and began "a tremendous and incessant firing . . . ," said surgeon Thacher. "The engines of war have raged with redoubled fury and destruction on both sides, no cessation day or night. . . ."

American and French soldiers with fixed bayonets charged one redoubt after another, with John Laurens and Alexander Hamilton leading a 400-man assault that captured the next-to-last outpost.

The men "bravely entered the fort with the point of the bayonet without firing a gun," declared Thacher, who tended the wounded. "We suffered the loss of eight men killed and about thirty wounded. . . ."

Cornwallis tried a wild nighttime escape across the York River, hoping that Banastre Tarleton and his dragoons could help lead the army north toward Maryland. But a sudden storm with gale-force winds prevented many of the soldiers from crossing, and Cornwallis ordered those who had already crossed to return to Yorktown.

Then the final bombardment began.

The British army in Yorktown thrashed about like a dying animal, turning first one way and then another in a desperate attempt to hide, but there was no place to hide from the rain of shells.

Cornwallis had had enough.

On October 17, at 9 A.M., a small, red-coated British drummer boy appeared on the parapet, beating his drum for a parley. The roaring of the cannons drowned out the sounds he made, but finally the Americans noticed him standing there.

"Had we not seen the red coat when he first mounted," said Lieutenant Ebenezer Denny, "he might have beat till doomsday." A ceasefire was arranged and the British surrendered. The silence that followed, declared Denny, was "the most delightful music to us all."

Two days later, as Washington and Rochambeau sat astride horses with their respective armies stretching for more than a mile behind them, the British marched out.

Cornwallis, pleading sickness, sent Brigadier General Charles O'Hara to surrender for him.

The conquered troops came out of Yorktown, said Doctor Thacher, "in a slow and solemn step, with shouldered arms, colors cased, and drums beating a British march. . . ."

The German troops came first and stacked their weapons neatly, but one American officer noticed that the British who came after them moved slowly and "appeared much in liquor."

Thacher said that many of them "manifested a sullen temper, throwing their arms on the pile with violence, as if determined to render them useless. . . ."

While some of the prisoners cried and others cursed, and the allied armies watched in silence, music from the British bands floated over the battlefield as the defeated soldiers played "The World Turned Upside Down."

British casualties were 596 killed and 8,081 captured, compared to French losses of 60 killed and 192 wounded, and American losses of 24 killed and 65 wounded.

One of the American wounded was a black soldier named Bristol Rhodes, who lost an arm and a leg.

To the end of his long life, Oliver Cromwell claimed to have seen the last man killed at Yorktown.

"The play, sir, is over — and the fifth act has just been closed," a jubilant Lafayette declared. "I was in a somewhat awkward situation during the first acts; my heart experienced great delight at the final one. . . ."

Cornwallis later visited Lafayette's headquarters and was amazed to see James Armistead, the man he had thought was *his* spy, in friendly conversation with the young Frenchman.

Armistead was not the only black man Lafayette praised for his help in defeating Cornwallis. James Robinson of Maryland, who had also fought at Brandywine, was given a gold medal by Lafayette for his valor at Yorktown (though there apparently is no record telling what he did).

When the Continental Army passed in review, wrote Baron Ludwig von Closen in his diary, the Black Regiment of Rhode Island was the "most neatly dressed, the best under arms and the most precise in all their maneuvers."

The Revolutionary War effectively ended on that day at Yorktown — October 19, 1781 — though a final peace treaty would not be ratified by Congress until April 15, 1783.

The United States of America had won its independence from England in the first revolution in modern times against a monarchy and an empire.

The victory had come none too soon, though. Congress was so broke its members had to contribute a dollar apiece to pay the express rider who brought them news of the victory.

It was not a victory for all Americans, however. One of the American military's first acts following the British surrender, was to place sentinels "all along the Beach" to prevent escaping slaves from reaching British ships.

And less than a week after the surrender, Washington established a guardhouse and ordered officers to place all black men and women in them until they could prove they were not slaves. He also ordered that advertisements for slaves be placed in newspapers so their owners could claim them (the same newspapers he and Jefferson sometimes used to advertise for their own escaped slaves).

In the meantime, Washington declared, the imprisoned African Americans were to be "sent into the Country to work for their Victuals and Cloathes."

Many of the Patriot soldiers who had fought to keep themselves and their loved ones from being "enslaved" by the English, now eagerly helped enslave black people.

United States naval authorities also helped enforce slavery. When an American privateer seized the British warsloop, the *Alert*, off Sandy Hook, New Jersey, the captain found that 11 of the 46 crewmen were black. A naval court gave the captain permission to auction off nine of the black sailors in a Trenton tavern.

Many Americans continued to demand that the new nation abolish slavery, however, and accept people of all races as equal citizens.

One of these efforts was initiated by an enslaved African American named Elizabeth Freeman, the widow of a soldier who died in battle. In 1781, Mrs. Freeman sued for her freedom and that of her daughter in a Massachusetts court, arguing that the state Bill of Rights said everyone in the nation was born free and equal, and that "she was certainly one of the nation."

The court agreed and set her free, along with her daughter.

When Elizabeth Freeman passed away almost 50 years later, the following inscription was carved on her gravestone: "She struck the death blow of slavery in Massachusetts."

John Laurens, who had never given up on his plan to free the slaves, was killed almost a year after Yorktown in a meaningless skirmish near the Combahee River in South Carolina. Only twenty-eight years old, he was one of the last casualties of the war.

Count Kosciuszko asked General Greene for permission to give Laurens's clothes to two black soldiers who were nearly naked, and Greene agreed.

"I have long deplored the wretched state of these men," Laurens had once written to his father, "and considered their history, the bloody wars excited in Africa to furnish America with Slaves — the groans of despairing multitudes toiling for the luxuries of merciless tyrants."

Even the failed attempt to help end slavery, Henry Laurens once told his son, "will, I know, afford you unspeakable satisfaction — The work . . . will at a future day be efficaciously taken up & then it will be remembered who began it in South Carolina."

When the British finally evacuated Savannah and Charleston in 1782, they took with them an estimated 20,000 escaped slaves along with several hundred free black men, women, and children. Historian Gary Nash has called the Revolutionary War "the largest slave uprising in our history."

Thousands of the slaves found freedom, but many were sold to slave owners in the British West Indies.

Many African Americans also sailed to freedom on French ships, much to the chagrin of Washington. Writing on behalf of a friend (Colonel William Fitzhugh) who had seen 40 of his slaves escape, including five who boarded a French ship, Washington told Count de Grasse: "I will take it as a very great favor if your Excellency will direct them to be sent back by any Vessel coming either to Virginia or Maryland."

French leaders, including de Grasse and Rochambeau, responded politely to Washington and other officials, but refused to return any slaves.

Congress even established the post of Commissioner

for Claims for Negroes, whose sole job was to help slave owners track down escaped slaves.

Lafayette had gone back to France a few weeks after the fall of Yorktown, but the slavery he witnessed in the United States continued to haunt him.

In February 1783, he wrote Washington "to propose a plan to you, which might become greatly beneficial to the black part of mankind. Let us unite in purchasing a small estate, where we may try the experiment to free the Negroes, and use them only as tenants. Such an example as yours might render it a general practice. . . . If it be a wild scheme, I had rather be mad in this way, then to be thought wise. . . ."

Washington told Lafayette that his plan was "a striking evidence of the benevolence of your heart. I shall be happy to join you in so laudable a work. . . ."

Washington never joined in the "laudable" work, however. Instead, he concentrated on retrieving as many escaped slaves as he could, including some of his own.

Washington was upset, he told the new British commander, Sir Guy Carleton, because some of his own runaway slaves "may probably be in New York," about to sail away with the British.

Carleton refused to return them, adding that he was "astonished" Washington thought the British would "be guilty of a notorious breach of the public faith towards people of any complexion. . . ."

Thomas Jefferson was also angry that the British refused to return slaves to their owners (including some of his) even though he knew the likely result would be execution, whipping, or other severe punishments for escaping.

Soldiers were now clamoring for their discharges, and some left without waiting to be discharged. All of them were still owed back pay, and a group of angry Pennsylvania recruits surrounded the Pennsylvania State House where Congress was meeting.

The delegates hurriedly fled to Princeton, and the recruits disbanded when they heard that a large force of Continental Army soldiers was marching against them.

Major John Armstrong wrote sarcastically that the delegates had "left a state where their wisdom has long been questioned, their virtue suspected, and their dignity a jest."

Finally it was time for the Continental Army to disband.

On November 3, 1783, all soldiers who had enlisted for the duration were discharged.

Oliver Cromwell received his discharge in the commander in chief's own handwriting, a fact "of which he was very proud, often speaking of it."

Cromwell was also "honored with the Badge of Merit for Six Years faithful service," and given a yearly pension. He would live to be one hundred years old.

Tobias Gilmore returned to his home in Taunton, Massachusetts, where he received a parcel of land and a cannon for his service. Every Fourth of July he hauled the cannon to Taunton Green and fired off 14 shots: one for each of the victorious colonies and a final one for George Washington.

Gilmore stopped his patriotic practice after he accidentally shot off a neighbor's arm one year.

Count Kosciuszko reportedly offered to take Agrippa Hull with him to Poland. Instead, Hull returned to his home in Stockbridge, Massachusetts, where he adopted the child of a runaway slave.

When Kosciuszko journeyed to the United States for a visit in 1797, Hull traveled to New York City where the two held an affectionate reunion. Perhaps they laughed about the time Kosciuszko unexpectedly returned to find Hull entertaining his friends in one of the Count's uniforms.

During this visit to the nation he had helped create, Kosciuszko was given a gift of land in Ohio. He ordered that the land be sold and the money used to start a school for black children.

John Peterson — who fought at Saratoga, escaped from the prison ship *Jersey*, and helped foil the *Vulture*'s attempt to pick up Major André after the officer's visit with Benedict Arnold — returned to Cortland, New York, to live in the house Colonel van Cortlandt had given him.

Peterson died at the age of one hundred and three, and his obituary declared that he had "the character of an honest man and a faithful soldier, and was much esteemed by all who knew him."

William Flora, who years later would volunteer to fight in the War of 1812, settled down once more in Portsmouth, Virginia. There he became a well-to-do businessman and property owner who was able to buy his wife and children out of slavery.

Barzillai Lew, who helped Ethan Allen capture Fort Ticonderoga and fought at Bunker Hill, married a young woman named Dinah Bowman and fathered a large family.

Lemuel Haynes, the Minuteman who heard "the shot heard round the world" at Lexington Green on that long-ago morning, went on to become an ordained minister who headed churches in Vermont and upstate New York. Haynes, the son of a white mother and black father, was one of the most popular ministers of his day.

And Jude "Old Rock" Hall, who first heard the sounds of battle at Bunker Hill, finally went back home to his family in Exeter, New Hampshire, after eight long years of fighting.

The African-American soldiers' deeds of valor had been acknowledged by most of those who had seen them in action.

"The Negroes make hardy soldiers," Alexander

Hamilton said, "and their bold efficiency in battle made officers, who frowned on them at first, learn that they were equal to any in the Army."

In his farewell address to the Black Regiment of Rhode Island, Lieutenant Colonel Edward Olney — who had taken command after Colonel Greene was killed — said he regretted that they had to "retire from the field without receiving any pay, or even their accounts settled and the balances due ascertained. . . ."

But, he added with "pride and pleasure," their wartime conduct had led him to hold them in "the most affectionate regard and esteem . . . which no time nor circumstances can eradicate. . . ."

And then the battle-weary veterans began the long walk home: hoping for the better tomorrow they had waited for so long, dreaming of building better lives for themselves and their loved ones in the new nation their blood and courage had helped create.

Freedom, Freeman, and Liberty were the names many black men gave themselves when they enlisted in the Continental Army. Such names were their own declarations of independence, announcing to the world that they expected to enjoy the freedom and liberty they were risking their lives to help white Americans enjoy.

And so they formed part of the backbone of the Continental Army, along with other Americans on the bottom rungs of society's ladder: recent Irish and German immigrants, unemployed "free white men on the move," laborers, and indentured servants.

Most black men apparently went willingly, viewing service in the army as a chance to stake their claim to equal American citizenship. They served an average of four and one half years, compared to an average of three and one half years for white soldiers. Several of the black men, including Jude "Old Rock" Hall, fought the entire eight years of the war.

The deeds of these black soldiers were as powerful an argument for equality as anyone could make, and for awhile it seemed that their dreams of equality would come true.

Abolition societies sprung up in the North and the South, and states throughout the North moved to abolish slavery. But this early progress was dealt a death blow with the drafting of the United States Constitution in 1787.

Southern slave owners, including George Washington and Thomas Jefferson, joined with Northern businessmen to write the protection of slavery into the Constitution: a protection John Quincy Adams described decades later as "morally and politically vicious."

"May Congress not say that every black man must fight? Did we not see a little of this last war?" Patrick Henry asked in arguing for the Bill of Rights. And once Congress passed such a law, he warned, it could also declare "that every slave who would go to the army should be free."

The Constitution and the Bill of Rights were thus adopted on the premise that slavery should be legally protected in the new nation, a decision that shocked and appalled the Marquis de Lafayette, Count Kosciuszko, and others who had risked their lives for American freedom — including the black soldiers. "I would never have drawn my sword in this cause of America could I have conceived that thereby I was founding a land of slavery," Lafayette wrote John Adams many years later.

In this political climate, several black Revolutionary War heroes were betrayed. Captain Mark Starlins, the Virginia pilot who had been so highly praised for his valor, died in slavery.

James Armistead, who took the name James Lafayette in honor of the man he so admired, was held in slavery for several years despite Lafayette's attempts to free him. The Virginia legislature finally emancipated Armistead, and when Lafayette returned to the United States in 1824, the two old comrades-in-arms held a joyful reunion.

James Robinson, who fought at Brandywine and was given a gold medal for his valor at Yorktown, was also re-enslaved after the war. He fought for the United States again in the War of 1812, and again was enslaved after the war ended.

Robinson, who was not freed until the Civil War, almost eighty years after the Revolution, died in Detroit in 1868 at the age of one hundred and fifteen.

"To his funeral, which was solemn, the population of Detroit flocked in great numbers," a newspaper reported, "in such wise making reparation for the injustice the veteran of so many battles had suffered in life."

Even some members of the Black Regiment of Rhode Island had to fight to keep from being re-enslaved by their former owners.

But black soldiers did not fight and die in vain in the Revolutionary War. Their valor gave black Americans their first strong foothold on freedom in this land, and brave men and women moved quickly to expand that foothold.

The free African American population grew larger than ever as a result of the war, and served as a beacon of hope to those still in slavery. This core of free people, mostly in the North, began building the churches, schools, and other institutions that would eventually help free their enslaved brothers and sisters.

In petition after petition in the decades following the war, black veterans backed their demands for racial equality and an end to slavery by reminding the nation of their service on the battlefields of the Revolutionary War.

"This is our home, and this is our country," said the delegates at one convention of black men. "Beneath its soil lies the bones of our fathers; for it, some of them fought, bled, and died. Here we were born, and here we will die."

Some black Revolutionary War veterans left legacies that would blossom long after their deaths. A man named Tom Burghardt, for instance, gained his freedom in return for fighting in the war.

He was thus able to start a family of independent, literate black descendants, culminating in the birth of his great-great-grandson: William Edward Burghardt

Du Bois, one of the greatest scholars the world has ever known.

But perhaps the greatest legacy of all from those 5,000 black heroes of the Revolutionary War was their belief that the eloquent words of the Declaration of Independence applied to all Americans:

"We hold these truths to be self-evident, that all men are created equal, that they are endowed by their Creator with certain unalienable Rights, that among these are Life, Liberty and the pursuit of Happiness. . . ."

And so the black veterans went forth in peace, as they had gone forth in war, determined to do everything in their power to make the dream come true: the dream that was the United States of America.

BIBLIOGRAPHY

BOOKS

Bennett, Lerone, Jr. *The Shaping of Black America*. New York: Penguin Books, 1993.

Bernstein, Barton J. *Towards a New Past: Dissenting Essays in American History*. New York: Pantheon Books, 1968.

Calloway, Colin G. *The American Revolution in Indian Country*. New York: Cambridge University Press, 1995.

Clarke, Clorinda. *The American Revolution, 1775–83: A British View*. New York: McGraw-Hill, 1967.

Cook, Frederic, ed. *Journals of the Military Expedition of Major General John Sullivan Against The Six Nations of Indians in 1779*. Ann Arbor: University Microfilms, 1967.

Dupuy, R. Ernest, and Dupuy, Trevor N. *An Outline History of the American Revolution*. New York: Harper and Row, 1975.

Flexner, James Thomas. *The Traitor and the Spy: Benedict Arnold and John Andre*. Boston: Little, Brown and Company, 1975.

Foner, Eric. *Tom Paine and Revolutionary America*. New York: Oxford University Press, 1976.

Freeman, Douglas Southall. *Washington*. New York: Charles Scribner's Sons, 1968.

Frey, Sylvia R. *Water From the Rock: Black Resistance in a Revolutionary Age*. Princeton: Princeton University Press, 1991.

Fulks, Bryan. *Black Struggle: A History of the Negro in America*. New York: Publishing Company, Inc., 1969.

Glasrud, Bruce A., and Smith, Alan M., eds. *Race Relations in British North America, 1607–1783*. Chicago: Nelson-Hall, Inc., 1982.

Garrison, William Lloyd; Moore, George Henry; and Wilkes, Laura Eliza. *The Negro Soldier: A Compilation*. Westport: Negro Universities Press, a division of Greenwood Press, 1970.

Greene, Robert Ewell. *Black Courage, 1775–1783*. Washington, D.C.: National Society of the Daughters of the American Revolution, 1984.

Gutman, Herbert G., ed. *Who Built America? Working People and the Nation's Economy, Politics, Culture and Society, Vol. 1*. New York: Pantheon Books, 1989.

Hibbert, Christopher. *Redcoats and Rebels: The American Revolution Through British Eyes*. New York: Avon Books, 1990.

Hosmer, James K. *Samuel Adams*. New York: Chelsea House, 1980.

Hughes, Langston. *Famous Negro Heroes of America*. New York: Dodd, Mead & Company, 1958.

Kaplan, Sidney, and Kaplan, Emma Nobrady. *The Black Presence in the Era of the American Revolution*. Amherst: University of Massachusetts Press, 1989.

Lauber, Almon Wheeler. *Indian Slavery in Colonial Times Within the Present Limits of the United States*. Williamstown: Corner House Publishers, 1970.

Leckie, Robert. *George Washington's War: The Saga of the American Revolution*. New York: HarperCollins, 1993.

MacLeod, Duncan J. *Slavery, Race and the American Revolution*. New York: Cambridge University Press, 1974.

Meltzer, Milton. *The American Revolutionaries: A History in Their Own Words, 1750–1800*. New York: Thomas Y. Crowell, 1987.

Nell, William C. *The Colored Patriots of the American Revolution*. Salem, N.H.: Ayer Company, Publishers, Inc., 1986.

Pearson, Michael. *Those Damned Rebels: The American Revolution as Seen Through British Eyes*. New York: G.P. Putnam's Sons, 1972.

Peckham, Howard H., ed. *The Toll of Independence: Engagements and Battle Casualties of the American Revolution*. Chicago: University of Chicago Press, 1974.

Quarles, Benjamin. *The Negro in the American Revolution*. New York: W.W. Norton and Company, 1973.

Ryan, Dennis P., ed. *A Salute to Courage: The American Revolution as Seen Through Wartime Writings of Officers of the Continental Army and Navy*. New York: Columbia University Press, 1979.

Scott, John Anthony. *Trumpet of a Prophecy: Revolutionary America, 1763–1783*. Alfred A. Knopf, Inc., 1969.

Sterling, Dorothy, ed. *We Are Your Sisters: Black Women in the Nineteenth Century.* New York: W.W. Norton and Company, 1984.

Trussell, John B.B., Jr. *Birthplace of an Army: A Study of the Valley Forge Encampment.* Harrisburg: Pennsylvania Historical and Museum Commission, 1976.

Wilson, Joseph T. *The Black Phalanx.* Salem, N.H.: Ayer Company Publishers, Inc., 1992.

Zinn, Howard. *A People's History of the United States: 1492–Present.* New York: HarperCollins, 1995.

JOURNALS

"Documents: Letters of George Washington Bearing on the Negro." *Journal of Negro History,* Vol. II (October 1917), pp. 411–422.

Greene, Lorenzo J. "Some Observations on the Black Regiment of Rhode Island in the American Revolution." *Journal of Negro History,* Vol. XXXVII (April 1952), pp. 142–172.

Harding, Vincent Gordon. "Wrestling Toward the Dawn: The Afro-American Freedom Movement and the Changing Constitution." *Journal of American History,* 74 (1987), pp. 718–739.

Hartgrove, W.B. "The Negro Soldier in the American Revolution." *Journal of Negro History* (1916), pp. 110–131.

Jackson, Luther P. "Virginia Negro Soldiers and Seamen in the American Revolution." *Journal of Negro History,* Vol. XXVII (July 1942), pp. 247–287.

Maslowski, Pete. "National Policy Toward the Use of Black Troops in the Revolution." *South Carolina Historical Magazine,* January 1972, pp. 1–17.

Norton, Mary Beth. "The Fate of Some Black Loyalists of the American Revolution." *Journal of Negro History,* Vol. LVIII (October 1973), pp. 402–426.

Ohline, Howard. "Slavery, Economics, and Congressional Politics, 1790." *Journal of Southern History,* 46 (1980), pp. 335–360.

Tilden, Robert J., translator. "The Doehla Journal," by Johann Conrad Doehla, one of the Hessian soldiers at the battle of Yorktown. *William and Mary Quarterly,* Vol. XXII (July 1942), pp. 229–274.

Windley, Lathan A. "Document: Runaway Slave Advertisements of George Washington and Thomas Jefferson." *Journal of Negro History,* Vol. LXIII (No. 4, Fall 1978), pp. 373–374.

INDEX

B

Banneker, Benjamin, 83
Barnet, Castel, 70
Barton, William, 71, 72
Battle, Shadrack, 70, 79, 96
Bayoman, Isaiah, 19
Beatty, Erkuries, 112
Bestes, Peter, 7
Beverly, Sylvester, 96
Bill of Rights, 169
Black, Primus, 26
Blackman, Epheram, 26
Blackman, Pomp, 19
Black Regiment of Rhode Island, 88–
    89, 97–98, 145, 155, 159, 167, 170
Black Samson, 76–77
Boardman, Cato, 19
Bonuses, recruitment and, 69
Boston, Massachusetts
    British evacuate, 45
    British occupy, 1, 2, 12, 26–27
    siege of, 23, 25, 44–45
Boston Massacre, 3–5
Boston Tea Party, 11–12
Bowman, Dinah, 166
Brant, Joseph (Thayendanegea, Mo-
    hawk chief), 112
Breed's Hill, Battle of, 22, 27–34
British army
    Americans joining, 101–102
    blacks and, 39, 40, 41, 42, 51, 99,
        100–101, 105, 114, 155–156
    Boston evacuated by, 45
    conditions in, 83, 84
    deaths in, 56, 64, 96, 110, 138,
        141–142, 158
    desertions from, 96, 139
    German mercenaries in, 50–51
    New York City attacked by, 51–53,
        54–60
    in South, 114, 119–120, 125
    strength of, 51–52, 154
British navy
    New York City campaign, 51–52
    Yorktown campaign, 152

Brooklyn, Battle of, 55–57
Brown, Caesar, 31
Buckner, Thomas, 108
Bunker's Hill, Battle of, 22, 27–34
Burghardt, Tom, 171–172
Burgoyne, John, 27, 80
Burr, Seymour, 31

C

Camden, South Carolina, Battle of,
    120–122
Camel, Thomas, 94–95
Campbell, Archibald, 101, 102
Campbell, William, 126, 127
Carr, Patrick, 4, 5
Carter, Isom, 114
Cavalry, 142–143
Charlton, Samuel, 95
Cherokee people, 111
Chester, John, 29
Cheswell, Wentworth, 80, 132
Christophe, Henri, 114
Cilley, Joseph, 94, 95, 96
Clark, Caesar, 79
Clark, Elijah, 102, 103
Clinton, Henry, 27, 28, 51, 91, 96, 99,
    105, 107, 120, 122, 124, 125, 128,
    142, 151, 153, 156
Closen, Ludwig von, 147, 159
Coburn, Primus, 115
Coburn, Titus, 31
Coercive Acts, 12
Collins, James, 127, 128
Colonial America
    revolts in, 1–2
    slave populations, 5
Common Sense (Paine), 46
Concord, Massachusetts, viii, 14, 15,
    16–17, 19–20, 23
Constitution (U.S.), slavery and,
    169–170
Continental Army. *See also* Militias
    blacks accepted in, 41–42, 44
    blacks excluded from, 37–41,
        43–44